100 IDEAS THAT
CHANGED ARCHITECTURE

Richard Weston

100 IDEAS THAT CHANGED ARCHITECTURE

Richard Weston

Laurence King Publishing

Introduction

This book's title poses two obvious questions: what is an architectural "idea," and how were the 100 ideas it discusses and illustrates chosen and organized? It will be readily apparent from the index that this is not a contribution to the burgeoning genre of architectural theory. Surprisingly few of the ideas are philosophical or theoretical in character; indeed, some readers may wonder whether some of them— like Fireplace with which the book begins, and Wall and Brick which quickly follow—are ideas at all.

This bias was as much of a surprise to the author as it may be to the reader, but it quickly became apparent when drafting a list of possible contents that the "ideas" that really change the practical art of architecture are not just the relatively few grand philosophical bodies of thought that shape civilizations, but frequently altogether more humble ideas like a brick or reinforcing concrete with rods of steel. Everything that humans make begins, ultimately, with an idea: not, perhaps, those we think of as patentable—the kind cartoonists like to represent as a bulb flashing in a scientist's head—but as a guiding concept that, for example, tells a stonemason how to shape and place stone on stone to create an arch which, as if by magic, makes it possible to defy gravity and make an opening in a wall. Many such ideas must have occurred independently to different people in different places and the moment when the metaphorical bulb first flashed will never be known—but this does not diminish their importance.

It takes only a few moments' reflection to realize that many of the most potent ideas that have changed architecture are of this seemingly prosaic character. One of the most celebrated in Modern architecture, the free plan, for example, would have been impossible without the development of central heating systems that liberated architects from the discipline of accommodating fireplaces and chimneys and, in time, teenagers from the constraints of continual parental supervision —just as the chimney had previously enabled the

development of grand houses with many private rooms or apartments.

The final selection of ideas was therefore made to reflect the varied character of the ones that have changed architecture in different ways. These include:

- elements of construction—wall, column and beam, vault, etc.—and architectural refinements of these, such as the Classical Orders of columns developed in ancient Greece, which some architects even today consider the most beautiful means of ordering architectural form;
- social ideas and innovations, ranging from the idea of the architect as an independent designer to such recent developments as community architecture and universal design (which used to be known as "design for the disabled");
- spatial types and means of organization, such as the Roman basilica, which became the pattern for most Christian churches, and the now ubiquitous corridor which is a surprisingly recent innovation;
- design/drawing techniques, both practical—such as the use of orthographic projection to create plans and sections, and computer-aided design techniques that has now almost completely replaced the drawing board—and conceptual, such as abstraction or layering;
- and, finally, those more idea-like ideas that have guided, explicitly or implicitly, the development of architecture, such as Humanism, thinking of a building as an organism, and some of the familiar slogans of modern architecture such as "form follows function" and "less is more."

The final selection aims to represent all these various types of idea, but it makes no pretense at completeness. The generic idea of a floor is discussed, as is its aggrandizement as a platform, but the roof is not—only those forms particular to masonry architecture, the vault and the dome, are given separate treatment. This reflects the book's bias toward Western architecture, which for most of its history was an architecture of stone, and also our desire to avoid any textbooklike endeavor to delimit a field that escapes all attempts at definition. We have also omitted what some might see as architecture's most basic idea—that of the room, or, more generally, "inside"—preferring to deal more empirically with various concrete means of enclosing space. This allows the idea of architecture as the "art of (enclosing) space" to appear in context when it first became the subject of discussion in the nineteenth century—and led, not long after, to the elimination of the traditional idea of the room, first in the work of Frank Lloyd Wright and then as a guiding principle of Modernist architecture embodied in Le Corbusier's famous "Five Points of a New Architecture."

Once the 100 ideas had been chosen, it was decided, after much discussion, to arrange them broadly chronologically, with the more prosaic ideas or technical means preceding the other kinds. This led, inescapably, to two broad clusters: the Renaissance revival of Classical Greek and Roman ideas and practices, which was destined to dominate Western architecture well into the nineteenth century; and the consequences of the Industrial Revolution, which changed the way we build and, in conjunction with related cultural developments, led to many of the key strands of recent architectural thought.

Most of the ideas reach through time and continue to shape our architecture. There is, inevitably, a slight bias toward including recent innovations and some discussed toward the end of the book—the fold springs to mind—may seem rather less important in a few years' time; or they may, courtesy of such novel digital techniques as parametric design, be far more widely influential than we might now anticipate.

Although the book's broadly chronological sequence will reward a linear reading from beginning to end, each short essay is intended to be complete and can be dipped into and, hopefully, enjoyed at random. Connections to other ideas are indicated by emboldening the relevant words, offering many alternative and—to borrow one of the ideas discussed—more Picturesque journeys of discovery. The discussion of architecture inevitably entails the use of some specialist vocabulary but this has been kept to a minimum; a short glossary explains a few technical terms that will be encountered along the way. Above all, this book is intended to be a widely accessible and engaging introduction to the broad spectrum of ideas that shape architecture.

IDEA № 1
FIREPLACE

Fire and human dwelling were inseparable in most climates until recently and the fireplace or hearth—source of heat and means of cooking—has been seen by many as the beginning of architecture. Fire was both practical necessity and social focus and the earliest known houses had fireplaces in the form of an open pit built into the ground.

This image illustrating February in a thirteenth-century medieval manuscript calendar from Laval, France, captures beautifully the primal human need for warmth in northern climates.

The smoke from such fires would escape inefficiently through holes in the roof. Despite the development of chimneys and **central heating** these early fire pits remained in use in rural houses well into the nineteenth century.

The Romans used ceramic tubes inside walls to draw smoke out of bakeries, but true chimneys—tall structures designed to draw gases and smoke up from the fire and disperse them into the atmosphere—did not emerge in Europe until the twelfth century. By the seventeenth century the chimney had become such an important feature that houses were frequently built around it, with a central stack acting as a supporting structure for one or more dwellings. In the late eighteeth century Count Rumford designed a fireplace with a tall, shallow firebox that was better at drawing the smoke up and out of the building and greatly improved the amount of radiant heat projected into the room. His design became the model for modern fireplaces.

Architecturally, the fireplace's focal role in a house or room, combined with the desirability of a fireproof surround, was celebrated with elaborately carved openings and surrounds. French châteaux such as Blois, Chambord and Fontainebleau (opposite) are known for the size and artistry of their chimneypieces, while in the Baroque and Rococo periods fireplaces were usually smaller but richer in decoration. The proliferation of fireplaces generated the picturesque roofscapes of great houses such as Burleigh in England, and socially its implications were even more significant: providing fireplaces throughout a dwelling made possible "a room of one's own," and the development of the modern sense of privacy and individuality.

Few modern homes have open fireplaces, due to the convenience of central heating and regulations on emissions, but gas fires and wood burners are still valued as a means of offering the ambience of a "real" fire. The fireplace, rather surprisingly, was valued by Le Corbusier as a powerful emblem of home, and even in his Unités d'Habitation he saw such a "sacred" focus as essential for a family "even if," as he put it, "the 'fire' comes courtesy of electricity." In Aalto's Villa Mairea (see p.148), heated by a form of air conditioning, a large white-plastered fireplace dominates the living spaces, recalling vernacular models. Frank Lloyd Wright's Prairie houses were organized around a central fire and the later, and cheaper, Usonian houses (see p.101), which had underfloor heating, similarly featured a focal fireplace that Wright considered "the psychological center of the home." In grander houses such as Fallingwater and Wingspread, a large chimney became the core around which Wright wrapped the entire dwelling, and a central fireplace and chimney were also famously deployed, with more than a trace of irony, in Robert Venturi's "Mother's House" (see pp.170–71): built for his mother in suburban Philadelphia in 1962 its deliberately "houselike" front was to become one of the most celebrated emblems of **Postmodernism**. ■

In Siena Cathedral, the floor is inlaid with colored stones to become part of the narrative that suffuses the whole structure.

Anchor to the earth

The Modernist love of continuity finds striking expression in OMA/Rem Koolhaas's Educatorium in Utrecht, where the ribbonlike floor and ceiling form an unbroken surface.

IDEA № 2

FLOOR

The earliest floors probably involved no more than clearing and enclosing a piece of ground, and of all the primary architectural elements the floor may appear most tied to constructional necessity and least amenable to formal manipulation. Yet although highly constrained, floors offer a surprising range of expressive opportunities.

They may extend beyond the building to form part of a raised **platform** or, as in the transformation of the Castelvecchio in Verona (1954–67, see pp.115, 150) by Carlo Scarpa, retreat from the enclosing walls so that the new interventions appear to "float" within the old construction. They may even, as in Le Corbusier's pilgrimage chapel at Ronchamp (1950–55), return to their origins as a surfacing of the ground as found, and thereby anchor the building decisively to locality and to Mother Earth.

Ground floors, like the "suspended" floors above them, may also be detached from the ground. When building with wood this is generally a practical necessity, to protect the floor from moisture, rain, or flood, and in many traditional Japanese buildings, in particular, necessity is celebrated by making the floor appear to float—an idea also exploited in Mies van der Rohe's flood-prone Farnsworth House (see p.154).

For practical and constructional reasons, most multistory buildings consist of a succession of similar floors. With masonry construction this followed structural logic, but while wood-framed buildings frequently had slightly projecting or "jettied" upper floors, it was only in the twentieth century that floors were treated as planes to be projected or rotated in order to establish a more dynamic relationship with their surroundings. Reflecting the new ideal of spatial continuity and exploiting **reinforced concrete** and **steel** construction, the floors of Frank Lloyd Wright's Fallingwater (1935, see p.61) are like suspended geological strata—an idea that Denys Lasdun would later explore as an urban strategy, notably in the National Theatre in London (1967–76).

The demands of furniture, posture, and **universal design** now demand that most floors be flat, horizontal, and free of frequent stepped changes of level. But with the introduction of the ramp in the Villa Savoye as the armature of an **architectural promenade** through the house, and in later projects such as the Strasbourg Congress Center and Firminy Church, where distinctions between floor and ramp became blurred, Le Corbusier instigated a train of thought that culminated in ongoing efforts—by Rem Koolhaas, Zaha Hadid, MVRDV, and others—to configure the primary circulation space of public buildings as a continuous, gently sloping floor.

Because we are in constant contact with them, directly or via furniture, the finishing of floors can crucially influence our experience of buildings. In Aalto's Säynätsalo Town Hall, for example, visitors enter on to a brick floor and rise via a brick stair, but on turning into the Council Chamber find themselves on highly polished wood which, more effectively than any written notice, urges stillness and silence. Here, as throughout his architecture, Aalto displays an awareness of our often subconscious responsiveness to materials that appears singularly lacking in many who deploy that recent addition to architecture's repertoire promoting visual continuity: the glass floor. ∎

In the Palazzo Rucellai in Florence Leon Battista Alberti emulated the Roman use of the Classical language as a means of articulating a wall as a structure of pilasters and columns. The incised stone joints we see are "ideal" forms, and do not correspond to the actual construction.

The articulation of space

IDEA № 3
WALL

Derived from the Latin word *vallum*, an earthwork that formed part of a Roman fortification system, the English word "wall" refers to any extended structure that encloses space or retains earth.

Conceived as an inhabited wall closing the village, Mario Botta's House in Ticino, Switzerland, uses colored concrete blocks to emulate the banded stone familiar from Italian Romanesque churches.

It is likely that such earth walls, tapered for solidity, were the model for one of the first great architectures to use the wall for monumental effect— that of ancient Egypt. In Greek architecture, by contrast, walls were secondary to the columns that were the primary elements of the ornamental **orders** and it fell to the Romans to turn the Greek system into a means of articulating the wall. The vast enclosing wall of the Colosseum in Rome (see p.25) is expressed as three tiers of arcades framed by half-columns in, successively, the Tuscan, Ionic, and Corinthian orders.

With the revival of interest in Roman architecture in early fifteenth-century Italy, the wall—which had been transformed into stone tracery by the Gothic masons—once again became a primary element of architectural expression. Nowhere is this more evident than in the Palazzo Rucellai in Florence (1446–51, opposite) by Leon Battista Alberti. Its basic expression was almost certainly derived from the Colosseum, with flat pilasters in the Tuscan and Corinthian orders above and below an order of Alberti's own invention, and the masonry is elaborated by clearly expressed joints, with heavily incised rustication at the ground floor to suggest strength. By no means all the joints we see, however, are "real" joints between stones in the actual masonry: what Alberti presents is a representation of an ideal wall, not simply a physical construction.

Alberti and other leading architects of the early Renaissance established an expressive language of the wall that came to dominate Western architecture.

Its range ran from the delicacy of Brunelleschi's Pazzi Chapel to the monumental power of Michelangelo's apses of St. Peter's in Rome. Stone walls might turn plastic in the hands of Borromini or be rendered with austere restraint by Palladio, but their preeminence was challenged only briefly by the Neoclassicists' return to Greek models, with their privileging of column over wall. It was not until technological developments in the nineteenth century began to displace masonry as the primary means of construction in large buildings that the wall's role came into question.

By freeing walls from their load-bearing function, the **structural frame** introduced new expressive possibilities such as **cladding** and the curtain wall. And walls in turn began to assume a new life, as freestanding planes that defined but no longer fully enclosed space: as such, they were crucial to the Modernists' redefinition of architectural **space** as a fluid continuum. Toward the end of the twentieth century, however, the masonry wall began to be reevaluated in the light of new environmental concerns: by absorbing the heat generated during the day and slowly releasing it at night, massive walls could act as a "thermal flywheel," reducing a building's dependence on energy systems. The practical and expressive potential of the wall in such **passive design** seems likely to be a major theme of architecture in the twenty-first century. ■

Ancient elements of building structure

IDEA № 4
COLUMN AND BEAM

The origins of column-and-beam systems of construction—the distant ancestors of modern **structural frames**—are generally traced back to the Neolithic trilithon, a rudimentary structure resembling a doorway and consisting of two large vertical stones supporting a third set horizontally across their tops.

In the final stage we know today this consists of five separate trilithons, surrounded by a circle of standing stones linked by stone lintels to form a continuous structure.

The presence of Mycenaean and Egyptian relics in burial sites at Stonehenge has led archaeologists to suggest overseas influence from the ancient Mediterranean civilizations. Among these none exploited the column-and-beam form on a grander scale than the Egyptians: the celebrated Great Hypostyle Hall of Karnak, for example, consisted of 134 columns in 16 rows; the middle two rows, higher than the others, were 33ft (10m) in circumference and 80ft (24m) high.

Stone's density and weakness in tension placed severe constraints on the distance that could be spanned by stone beams, and while the Greeks concentrated on the exquisite formal refinements in developing the **Classical Orders**, it fell to the Romans to exploit compressive structures, using the **arch** and **vault**, more suited to masonry construction. In the Far East, however, wood was the preferred material for monumental architecture, and beams could be made to span far greater distances.

Central to the Chinese system of building that influenced countries throughout the Far East was the *dougong*, a structural element of interlocking wooden brackets. Widely used from the seventh century BC onward, and brought to a peak in the Tang and Song periods, these bracket sets joined columns to beams and consisted of precisely cut elements that locked together without glue or fixings. They provided a degree of flexibility that is thought to have helped the buildings resist earthquakes, but after the Song period their elaboration on palatial and religious buildings became increasingly ornamental.

The roof members supported by the *dougong* consisted of either large beams —roughly squared tree trunks—or rudimentary trusses formed of rectilinear layers of beams. The Chinese showed no interest in technological innovations that characterized later Western architecture, and although the Greeks used a rudimentary form of truss to roof their temples, it was the Romans who overcame the limitations on span imposed by lumber sizes by developing roof trusses reminiscent of those we know today: the largest of all, covering the throne room of the emperor Domitian (81–96 AD), had a width of 104ft (31.67m).

Structurally, major advances in column-and-beam systems came with

the development of **structural frames** using **reinforced concrete** and **steel**. Both allowed the material to be shaped in response to the forces at work: with columns and beams, most of the structural "work" is done by the material farthest from the section's center—hence the steel I, channel, and hollow sections that began to be standardized at the end of the nineteenth century and are now used in building structures worldwide. ■

Steel frames, consisting of vast networks of columns and beams, have been the preferred structure for tall building in the U.S. since the late nineteenth century.

Threshold of entrances and exits

IDEA № 5

DOOR

"A door," observed the Dutch architect Aldo van Eyck, "is a place made for an occasion." The language is personal, but the thought universal: although necessary for security, privacy, and climatic protection, doors transcend the demands of function by mediating the moment of entering and leaving a building or room.

Consider the contrast between entering through an imposing large pair of double doors that swing open courtesy of doormen, with the now familiar experience of pushing against the resistance of an automatic door closer demanded by fire regulations.

Physically, doors have changed remarkably little since the first evidence of their use in ancient Egypt, where the door's symbolic significance was touchingly made evident by painting doorways to the world after death inside tombs. The most common forms of modern door—swing (courtesy of pivots, hinges coming later); sliding; and multipanel folding—were all in use in ancient Greece and Rome. Even the first automatic door is surprisingly old: activated by a foot-sensor it was installed in the royal library during the reign of Emperor Yang of Sui (604–18).

Most doors were made of wood, but metals, especially bronze, became popular for aristocratic and public buildings. In Renaissance Italy architects generally relied on the door casing to impress, but in the France of the Sun King, Louis XIV, and in Germany the pattern was reversed, with elaborately carved doors replete with columns and pediments set in plain walls.

New materials, such as laminated or toughened glass, brought variations on these familiar forms but it was only with the invention of the revolving door—patented in Philadelphia in 1888 by Theophilus Van Kannel—that a genuinely new type appeared. Although valuable for eliminating the need for a two-door draft lobby to keep heat in a building, the revolving door was invented to overcome another practical problem: the tendency in tall buildings for the upward flow of warm air to create negative pressure, making swing doors hard to open.

The emphasis on the continuity of **space** in the **International Style**, often led to doors that were understated rather than celebrated, made of glass or appearing as an abstract plane of color in a glass wall, and the traditional change of level marked by the doorstep was often eliminated—anticipating the level access for wheelchairs which would later be required by the principle of **universal design**.

The postwar reevaluation of Modernist aspirations rehabilitated the door as a site of architectural invention—and nowhere, arguably, more subtly than in a Roman Catholic church by Aldo van Eyck in The Hague. Arriving individually or in family groups, churchgoers enter through an inward-opening single door of normal width; leaving en masse as a congregation they depart through a much wider door; set into the opening, the narrower door lies just a few inches behind the larger, and between these two solid planes of wood a strip of glass gives a glimpse in and out. The human-scale pass doors found in the grand doors of castles and palaces may have been an inspiration, but as a place

made for the occasions of entering and leaving it has few recent rivals. ■

OPPOSITE: *"Places made for an occasion": from Gaudí's Casa Milà in Barcelona and Michel de Klerk's housing in Amsterdam (top left and top center) to medieval doors in San Gimignano (bottom right and this page above), the design of openings and doors offers rich, expressive possibilities.*

Eyes of the building

WINDOW

Windows are sources of light and fresh air, but they are also the "eyes of the building," framing our experience of the wider world and, more perhaps than any other architectural element, giving character to a building.

BELOW: In the intense southern light of Florence a tiny window is sufficient to fill this cell in the monastery of San Marco with light.

From rudimentary holes covered with animal hides or cloth, wood, or paper, via the Roman introduction of cast **glass**, windows blossomed in the Gothic architecture of Europe. Lacking large sheets of glass, vast openings were framed by traceries of stone and made by joining pieces of colored glass with lead cames to create a light that transformed the interior into a vision of heaven.

During the High Renaissance in Italy and France, window openings became key elements of architectural composition. Vertical rectangles conforming to Classical **proportions**, they were typically divided by a single mullion and transom forming a cross and decorated with architraves, cornice, and pediment and, later, framing pilasters. During the Baroque period these decorative window enclosures—like **doors** and **fireplaces** —were elaborately scrolled and ornamented with fantastic cartouches, consoles, masks, and human figures.

In England's less intense light, Renaissance architecture was reinterpreted as planar surfaces dominated by window openings, most famously in Robert Smythson's Hardwick Hall— "more glass than wall" as a contemporary wit is said to have observed. Such use of glass was as much a statement of wealth as of architectural taste, and when glass appeared in ordinary seventeeth-century homes William III introduced a window tax—possibly giving rise to the expression "daylight robbery." Larger, vertically sliding sash

windows eventually became widespread in England and Holland, athough French designers probably played a key role in their invention. Sash windows reached their apogee in Georgian architecture, and with their splayed reveals and delicate, subtly molded wooden subdivisions provided an exquisite quality of light.

The twentieth century brought major technical developments in glass and window framing—aluminum and steel, and later the practical but ugly UPVC became widespread—but architecturally traditional windows were at odds with the "honest" expression of frame construction and the urge toward spatial continuity. These prompted innovations such as the curtain wall and ribbon windows—the latter one of Le Corbusier's **Five Points of a New Architecture**.

True to modernity's other face—a fascination with the primitive and an urge to return to origins—some of the most memorable modern windows sprang from the desire to recapture the primal act of making a hole in a wall. The studied but seemingly random scatter of windows across the south wall of Le Corbusier's chapel at Ronchamp drew inspiration from North Africa, while in St. Peter's Church at Klippan in Sweden, Sigurd Lewerentz evoked a cavelike atmosphere by providing minimal light and placing frameless glazing across the outside of, rather than within, the window openings. Emulated by Jørn Utzon in Can Lis

(opposite bottom), his home perched on a cliff in Majorca, this idea yielded windows framed by deep stone reveals that make the drama of sea and sky integral to the room. ■

Recessed, set flush with the wall, or projecting as a shallow bay, windows are a primary expressive element of architecture as well as a means of lighting the interior and framing views—seen to dramatic effect in Jørn Utzon's house, Can Lis, in Majorca (opposite bottom).

"When you are designing a window, imagine your girlfriend sitting inside looking out." —*Alvar Aalto*

The basic building block

BRICK

The brick is a cheap, portable building unit that fits in the human hand. The first bricks may well have been formed by hand-shaping cracked earth from the mud deposited across the flood plains of the Nile, Tigris, or Euphrates.

Designed by Peder Vilhelm Jensen-Klint, the Grundtvig Church in Copenhagen (1913–40) fuses a modern Expressionist style with a version of Gothic drawn from rural churches. Built almost entirely of standard yellow Danish bricks— some six million were required, allegedly none of them cut—its "honest" construction became an exemplar for many Danish architects.

The earliest known permanent dwellings, dating from around 8300 BC, were built with loaf-shaped mud bricks whose upper surfaces were indented to key in the mud mortar: modern bricklayers would be in no doubt about how to lay them. The first artificially fired bricks were produced in Mesopotamia around 3000 BC but cheaper, sundried ones remained in general use and were the commonest material in Rome until imperial times.

Kiln-firing freed brick production from the constraints of a suitable climate, and the craft of brickmaking spread with the Roman legions, taking root throughout Europe wherever suitable clay deposits were available. It died out during the Dark Ages but was revived in the twelfth century: the early medieval boom in religious building in England required vast quantities of bricks, and while many were plundered from Roman remains, brickworks became common. In Spain, following the Moorish invasion, Islamic brick-building techniques mingled with those of Rome, and lived on long after the Reconquest.

The modern form of brick was invented around the mid-twelfth century, probably in northern Germany, and is shorter and thicker than the long, flat Roman type. The strongest and most decorative form of bonding—Flemish bond, laid with alternating headers and stretchers— was invented in the Low Countries; in Holland, with its dearth of native stone, brick dominated all other materials. A seventeenth-century Dutch kiln could produce more than 600,000 bricks in a single firing, and only in the nineteenth century, when the mechanical extrusion and pressing of bricks replaced hand-molding, and the continuous tunnel kiln was introduced, was the rate dramatically increased.

For all its versatility and weathering qualities, brick has generally been regarded as the poor relation of stone. Both Vitruvius and Alberti commended its use, but Renaissance architects generally emulated Roman precedents and faced their brick walls with plaster or stone. The latter was, of course, usually more costly and therefore carried greater prestige, and both offered the even surfaces required by the Classical emphasis on **form**.

For many Modernists brick was representative of the "old" architecture and it was not until after the Second World War, with the completion of buildings such as Alvar Aalto's Säynätsalo Town Hall (1949–52) and Le Corbusier's Jaoul houses (1954–56), that brick was rehabilitated as a viably "modern" material. It was, however, used in the 1920s in several houses by Mies van der Rohe and in his seminal project for a Brick Villa (1923), where "truth to materials" was observed by using the brick as a **module**. ∎

The Great Ziggurat of Ur (in present-day Iraq) was finished in the twenty-first century BC and reconstructed in the sixth century BC. One of the largest surviving ancient brick structures, it consists of a three-layered solid mass of mud brick faced with burnt bricks set in bitumen. The facade of the lowest level and the monumental staircase were rebuilt under Saddam Hussein.

Flight to another level

IDEA № 8
STAIRCASE

The first true stairs almost certainly developed from wooden ladders and were made as straight flights of the kind still widely found in domestic architecture. The so-called "dog-leg" (or U-shaped) stair that is now ubiquitous in multistory buildings was common in Roman architecture but fell out of favor in medieval Europe where the spiral, or more correctly helical, stair was common.

Although now relatively uncommon, helical stairs seem to be of surprisingly ancient origin; a "winding stair" is mentioned in the Old Testament as one of the delights of Solomon's Temple.

Among architects and theorists stairs have provoked surprisingly disparate reactions. Vitruvius drew attention to their danger and Alberti saw them as a nuisance to be accommodated rather than an opportunity for architectural expression. Vasari and Scamozzi, by contrast, likened them to the veins and arteries of the body, while Palladio praised their beauty. His *Quattro Libri* illustrate several helical stairs, including a spectacular design consisting of four independent but interlocking ones, but in his villas the stairs were generally of modest design.

Palladio created nothing to rival the spectacular helical stair by Vignola in the Villa Farnese in Caprarola, still less the diminishing perspective of Bernini's tunnel-vaulted Scala Regia in the Vatican or the surging masonry of Michelangelo's stair into the Laurentian Library. By contrast with the generally understated stairs of Palladio's villas, English country houses generally made a grand stair hall the focus of the spatial **composition**.

The contemporary concern with the importance of stairs as a means of escape in case of fire—a key determinant of modern building plans—can be traced back to a series of major fires in Europe in the 1840s. As a direct response, Gottfried Semper's Vienna Burgtheater, completed in 1888, included no less than seven enclosed, fire-protected stairs. Safety concerns also seem to have prompted renewed interest in stairs' expressive possibilities, nowhere more spectacularly than in Charles Garnier's Paris Opera (1857–74, see pp.88–89), where the flow of people up and around the circulation system to the theater's many levels offers performances to rival those on stage. A similar interest in the "theater" of movement informed Le Corbusier's conception of the **architectural promenade**, although where possible he favored the leisurely movement up a ramp to the more rapid ascent offered by stairs—an idea taken to an extreme by the helical ramp of Frank Lloyd Wright's Guggenheim Museum in New York (see p.128). Prior to this Wright had generally suppressed the diagonals of staircase balustrades, which he saw as being at odds with the horizontality of his designs.

Despite the ubiquity of **elevators**, stairs are still central to orchestrating movement through many public buildings, above all theaters and concert halls, and two twentieth-century examples—Hans Scharoun's Philharmonie in Berlin and Jørn Utzon's Sydney Opera House—define their expressive range. In the former, Scharoun deploys a multiplicity of "hanging" stairs, landings, and balconies, whereas in Sydney Utzon leads visitors up and across a series of levels that seem to be carved out of the ground—recalling what were, perhaps, the earliest stairs of all, cut into sloping land by repeated footfalls. ∎

LEFT: *In love with horizontal "earth lines," Frank Lloyd Wright articulated this stair into the plunge pool below his Fallingwater House into a series of concrete planes and slender steel hangers.*

Most staircases are designed to facilitate easy movement between floors. Here at the Wurzburg Residenz in Germany, however, the shallow pitch imposes a slow, stately ascent, allowing time to contemplate the Tiepolo ceiling.

IDEA № 9

CLASSICAL ORDERS

The origins of the Classical Orders in ancient Greece is still the subject of debate among scholars, but their importance to the history of Western architecture can hardly be overstated. As the word "orders" implies, their significance goes far beyond a particular type or proportion of column, embracing an entire system of order analogous to the pitch, duration, and harmony of notes in classical music.

The Greeks invented three orders—the Doric, Ionic, and Corinthian; the Romans added an unfluted version of the Doric known as Tuscan, and a fused Ionic and Corinthian order known as the Composite. Despite many later attempts to create "national" orders—notably in France—these five became the basis of the Classical language learned and used by successive generations of architects well into the twentieth century.

The refinement of the Greek orders was based on binary formal oppositions—protruding vs. indented, straight vs. curved—and a system of tripartition that applies at every scale, from overall composition to detail: the orders themselves consist of an entablature (the part that rests on the column); the column; and the plinth or stylobate (the part on which the column rests). The entablature is further subdivided (from top to bottom) into cornice, frieze, and architrave. The Doric is a partial exception to the principle of tripartition, in that the Greek version lacked a plinth, but the articulation of its convex circular shaft into 20 concave flutes and its subtle vertical swelling or *entasis* exemplify the unsurpassed beauty of the Greek models.

The idea that the orders originated as stone imitations of wooden structures is ancient—Vitruvius's discussion of the **"primitive hut"** would find many emulators—and is now widely accepted by scholars. It was, however, vigorously rejected by advocates of architecture as the "art of building" such as Viollet-le-Duc who saw Greek temples as refined examples of masonry **column-and-beam** structures. In ancient Greece columns were always used as free-standing structural elements, but the Romans introduced the idea of deploying them as a means of organizing a building's facade by using "engaged" columns that formed part of the wall, or by flattening them to create low-relief pilasters.

The Roman use of the orders emphasized both their "ordering" and ornamental character and was much emulated in the Renaissance and later Classical architecture. It was, however, seen as a major departure from "true" Classical principles by eighteenth-century Neoclassicists who advocated a return to the "pure," structurally clear buildings of ancient Greece.

As well as offering a system for organizing a composition the Classical Orders were also a means of giving it character. Vitruvius famously associated the proportions of the columns with the human body—the "sturdy" Doric was male and the Ionic female, while the slender Corinthian was associated with a young "maiden" —and the orders were deployed according to accepted conventions to give a character, or sense of decorum, appropriate to a building's status and purpose. This idea of character derived from Aristotle's theory of human nature in which it was seen as an expression of moral purpose—not, as now, of individual traits but of typical ones—hence the shock felt by many when Palladio used Greek temple fronts on private villas. ∎

The original three Greek orders consisted, from right to left, of the Doric, Ionic, and Corinthian. The Romans added the Tuscan—a more "primitive" unfluted version of the Doric—and the Composite, which combined the Ionic and Corinthian capitals eventually followed in the Renaissance, completing the five Classical Orders.

The influential idea of using the orders to organize a wall was introduced by the Romans. Here, on the Colosseum in Rome, engaged Tuscan, Ionic, and Corinthian columns are deployed on the lower three stories, while the attic story features flat Corinthian pilasters.

"The Gothic system permitted a lightening of masonry structures."

By enabling designers to vary the ratio of width to height, the Gothic system of pointed arches and vaults, seen here in early and pure form at Amiens Cathedral, revolutionized the possibilities of masonry architecture.

Basic unit of the dome and vault

IDEA № 10
ARCH

The arch was known to builders in several ancient civilizations but, for reasons that are not clear, its use was confined to utilitarian or underground structures such as storehouses or drains. It reached its apogee in the Gothic but was uncommon in Modern architecture.

The arch enables the spanning of spaces or making of openings in masonry walls because, in principle, it is a pure compression structure and therefore ideally suited to materials such as stone and brick that are strong in compression but weak in tension. An arch does, however, generate outward thrusts at its base, which must be resisted to ensure stability.

The ancient Romans were the first to exploit the architectural potential of the arch. It formed the basis of the imposing bridges, aqueducts, and viaducts that accompanied the expansion of the Roman Empire and enabled Rome to become the first metropolis with a population of more than a million. Arched openings, ranged in tiers of **arcades**, were deployed on structures like the Colosseum (see p.25), and triumphal arches celebrated major military victories. Extruded, the arch formed **vaults**, and rotated it enabled the construction of **domes**.

Despite the vast size to which they pushed it, the semicircular arch used by the Romans—and later revived in the Romanesque architecture of Europe's first wave of church and monastic building—had two serious limitations: it generated substantial outward thrusts and, as the basis of a system of vaulting, could only be used to generate square cross-vaults. These issues were addressed by the introduction of the Gothic pointed arch, which reduced the outward thrusts and, because its vertical and horizontal dimensions could be varied independently, allowed the vaulting of rectangular bays. The Gothic system permitted a lightening of masonry structures; to cope with the remaining unresolved thrusts masons developed elaborate systems of buttresses.

The strongest forms for arches are given by parabolic and catenary curves. These formed the basis of the Catalan system of vaulting exploited by Antoni Gaudí, who derided buttresses as "architectural crutches," and later by the Venezuelan engineer Eladio Diaste.

Arches were not widely used in Modern architecture, partly because of the availability of materials such as steel and reinforced concrete strong in both compression and tension, partly because the temporary centering needed for their construction is expensive, and partly because they appeared less "modern." They did, however, make a monumental return in the work of Louis Kahn, who introduced thin reinforced concrete ties to resist the outward thrusts and, in brick buildings in India and Bangladesh, deployed upside-down arches as a novel means of resisting the upward thrusts generated by earthquakes. ■

The spanning of space

IDEA № 11

VAULT

The simplest forms of vault are produced by extruding or rotating a semicircular arch: the former is a barrel vault, the latter a **dome**. Like a masonry arch, a pure barrel vault needs wooden centering to support it during construction.

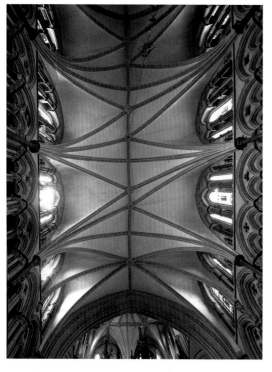

Lincoln Cathedral is celebrated for its experimental vaults, such as that seen here in St. Hugh's Choir—known as the "Crazy Vault" on account of its eccentric, asymmetrical version of the classic six-part tierceron vault developed in France.

Some of the oldest examples of vaults, for granaries at Thebes in Egypt, built c.1250 BC, have an elliptical form resulting from an ingenious way of building that eliminated the need for temporary works. A similar system, using bricks and clay tiles cemented with mortar, was used c. AD 550 to build the majestic catenary arch vault over the great hall at Ctesiphon (opposite).

The first major innovation in vaulting, the groin vault, results from the intersection of two semicircular vaults of the same diameter: their lines of intersection are elliptical and known as groins, and it is down them that the load is transmitted, allowing the vault to be supported on four piers rather than walls (although an outward thrust must still be accommodated). Groin vaults were developed on a vast scale by the Romans and, exploiting the geometric freedom of the pointed arch, Gothic masons made many innovations in rib vaulting using both the Roman quadripartite form, and a new sexpartite form that reconciled the differing bay widths of nave and aisles. These underpinned an array of visually complex forms based on the proliferation of decorative ribs, but it was only the English fan vault that represented a structural advance. Its strength came from a doubly curved surface, not the ribs that delineated the flow of forces, and in this it anticipated modern systems.

Notable among these is the Catalan brick-vaulting tradition based on overlapping laminations of thin, fired-clay tiles. Although ancient in principle, its potential was radically enlarged in the late nineteenth century by Rafael Guastavino's application of graphical means of statical analysis. His ideas were taken up by Antoni Gaudí and, in Venezuela, by the engineer Eladio Diaste who, sensing the economy and beauty that can result from aligning the elements of a structure along the lines of force, built pure compression vaults spanning up to 177ft (54m), and gravity-defying cylindrical barrel shells that act in compression across their curves and as beams longitudinally.

Major developments in vaulting came with the refinement of thin-shell and grid-shell systems. A pioneer of both was the Russian Vladimir Grigoryevich Shukhov (1853–1939), whose eight thin-shell pavilions for the All-Russia Exhibition of 1896 covered an area of 291,000ft² (27,000m²). No one pushed such structures to more dramatic limits than the Spanish-born engineer-architect Félix Candela (1910–97), who emigrated to Mexico in 1939 and attracted worldwide attention with the Cosmic Ray Pavilion at the Ciudad Universitaria near Mexico City. The reinforced concrete roof varies in thickness from only ½in (1.6cm) to 2in (5cm). From 1953 to 1955, Candela built the Church of La Virgen Milagrosa (The Miraculous Virgin) in Mexico City with a warped roof of reinforced concrete just 1½in (3.8cm) thick. ∎

The spectacular 85ft- (26m-) span stone vault of Taq-I, part of the imperial palace complex at Ctesiphon in modern-day Iraq, is among the largest to have survived from the ancient world.

The archetypal building "crown"

DOME

The dome is one of the oldest and most universal of structural forms. Like semicircular arches, all domes exert an outward thrust.

Remains of corbeled domes made of mammoth tusks and bones dating back up to 20,000 years have been found in the Ukraine and "true" mud-brick domes from c.6000 BC excavated in Mesopotamia. The architectural history of the dome, however, begins with the Romans who built them of stone, brick, and concrete. The latter enabled the construction of the Pantheon in the second century AD. Like semicircular arches, all domes exert an outward thrust: in the Pantheon (opposite) this was resisted by 20ft- (6m-) thick brick walls, and in St. Peter's—when evidence of spreading appeared—by heavy iron chains.

In the religious buildings of the Eastern Roman Empire domes were frequently used over the square crossings of **basilican** churches. Initially the awkward junction between dome and square was resolved by corbeling or by "squinch" arches, but eventually, in the most celebrated of Byzantine churches, the Hagia Sophia in Constantinople (built 532–37 and now a mosque in the modern Istanbul), this was elegantly resolved by the use of sections of dome, known as pendentives, to fill the triangular space between the dome edge and supporting structure. Byzantine architects also introduced a cylindrical drum with windows between the pendentives and dome. Both forms were widely emulated in the Renaissance, and Byzantine models are also thought to have inspired the use of domes in Islamic building, the Dome of the Rock in Jerusalem being the earliest survivor.

Spatially, the centralized, circular space described by a dome was at odds with the axial progression from west front to altar required by the Christian liturgy, and the resolution of this dilemma led to an innovation that was central to Baroque architecture, namely the oval dome. The first was built by Vignola for the chapel of Sant' Andrea in Via Flaminia in Rome and the form was brilliantly exploited by Bernini and Borromini.

Dome construction in the twentieth century was transformed by new materials such as reinforced concrete and steel. Thin "eggshell" domes of prestressed concrete were pioneered by the great Italian architect-engineer Pier Luigi Nervi (1891–1979), among others, while the invention of the geodesic dome—a spherical or part-spherical shell structure or lattice shell based on a network of great circles (geodesics)—offered unprecedented lightness.

Geodesic domes were pioneered in Germany after the First World War but are generally associated with Richard Buckminster Fuller (1895–1983), who received an American patent for the structural principle and became an enthusiastic advocate of its ability to enclose space with a minimal amount of material. Thanks to Fuller's cult status in the American counterculture of the late 1960s geodesic domes found favor for temporary drop-out homes—two DIY "Domebooks" were produced —and, ironically, were also used by the military as air-liftable temporary shelters. Problematic at small scale—door openings were notoriously awkward, and waterproofing problematic—geodesic domes found occasional large-scale use, spectacularly so in the Fuller-designed U.S. Pavilion at the Montreal Expo of 1967 (right top). ■

TOP: *Designed by Richard Buckminster Fuller as the U.S. Pavilion for the 1967 Montreal Expo, this 249ft- (76m-) diameter geodesic dome was built with steel struts and acrylic cladding. It is now used as a biosphere in the city's environmental museum.*

ABOVE: *Built by the engineer Pier Luigi Nervi for the 1960 Rome Olympic Games, the Palazzetto dello Sport featured a ribbed concrete dome that, from the inside, appeared almost to float on a ring of light.*

"The architectural history of the dome begins with the Romans."

Built in the second century AD during the reign of Emperor Hadrian, the dome of the Pantheon in Rome was a tour de force of concrete construction, and at 142ft (43.4m), the span was only surpassed in 1469 with the completion of Brunelleschi's dome

The Saint-Hubert Gallery in Brussels, Europe's second covered arcade, built shortly after London's Burlington Arcade, offered luxury shopping and the pleasures of "outdoor" cafés in a northern city.

Rhythmic arched walkway

IDEA № 13

ARCADE

An arcade denotes three distinct but related elements in architecture: a series of **arches** supported by columns or piers; a passageway between arches and a wall; or a covered—generally glazed—walkway giving access to stores. Structurally, as the slender piers of surviving Roman aqueducts confirm, an arcade is highly efficient because the outward thrusts of the successive arches press against each other and need no buttressing.

TOP: *The Piazza Maggiore is a focus of Italy's "city of arcades," Bologna.*

ABOVE: *Filippo Brunelleschi's Ospedale degli Innocenti (Foundling Hospital) in Florence, an early Renaissance masterpiece, addresses the adjacent square with a generous, elegantly light arcade.*

The Romans also used arcades to build large walls, as seen at the Colosseum in Rome (see p.25), where each of its three stories is articulated by arcaded openings framed by columns attached to piers, and the whole is surmounted by a heavy, blind story to give stability. The later form of arches resting on columns was extensively used in Romanesque, Gothic, and Renaissance architecture, and Gothic builders also used "blind" arcades decoratively to articulate wall surfaces and frame niches for sculpture.

The arcade as a covered passageway also dates back to Roman times. Medieval cloisters were generally arcaded, as were the secluded courtyards of mosques. Italian Renaissance towns such as Bologna (right top) boast extensive networks of arcades lining stores and other buildings, but it was only in the nineteenth century that the glazed arcade we identify with shopping emerged. The pioneer was Lord Cavendish who, having inherited Burlington House in London (now home to the Royal Academy of Arts), decided to connect Piccadilly and Burlington Gardens with a covered route "for the sale of jewellery and fancy articles of fashionable demand." Burlington Arcade opened in 1819 and consisted of a straight, top-lit walkway lined with 72 small, two-story units.

The Burlington's first successor, the 699ft- (213m-) long Saint-Hubert Gallery (opposite) in Brussels opened in 1847, operating under the motto *Omnibus omnia* (Everything for everybody) displayed on its palacelike facade. Brilliantly lit, its luxurious ambience was created by leading fashion retailers.

As an urban element arcades were frequently used as a profitable means of opening up neglected land locked within urban blocks, or of connecting major destinations—much like the "magnet" stores placed at the ends of modern shopping malls. Arguably the most splendid of all arcades—the Galleria Vittorio Emanuele II in Milan (1861–77)—connects the city's cathedral to the La Scala opera theater and, as a precursor of the modern mall, has lent the name Galleria to many later, architecturally less distinguished shopping centers.

In Paris an extensive network of arcades was introduced as part of Baron Haussmann's renovation of the city under Napoleon III (1852–70). This fostered the street life that is widely regarded as the first manifestation of an identifiably modern lifestyle, epitomized by the strolling *flâneur* whose preoccupation with casual experiences and encounters in the modern city fascinated the poet Charles Baudelaire. The arcades became the focus of the German critic Walter Benjamin's (1892–1940) unfinished *Passagenwerk* ("The Arcades Project"). Preoccupied by what he called the "commodification of things" in the bustling arcades, Benjamin saw in the merging of street and interior the fragmentation of historical time into ephemeral displays and kaleidoscopic distractions. ∎

Arranging rooms around a private outdoor space

Modeled on the cloisters of medieval monasteries, the colleges of Oxford University form a network of courtyards—or "quads" as they are known locally.

IDEA № 14

COURTYARD

Archaeological evidence suggests that many of the earliest known houses consisted of a room with a central fire and a hole in the roof to allow smoke to escape. It seems likely that this was the catalyst for one of the abiding spatial types in architecture: by placing the fire in an outdoor space surrounded by a doughnut-shaped room, the courtyard was born.

Courtyards as we know them date from around 3000 BC in China and Iran. In ancient Rome, where the courtyard was called the **atrium**—a term that now generally describes a glass-covered interior space—houses formed single-story, windowless terraces along streets, with the atrium as the principal source of light, air, and—thanks to a central pool—water. Larger homes also included a garden surrounded by colonnades, which turned it into a second courtyard, providing the model for both the monastic cloisters of medieval Europe and the *cortile*, or arcaded court, of Renaissance palazzi in Italy.

Courtyard houses were widely adopted throughout the Islamic world and typically arranged as continuous "mats" of introverted flat-roofed buildings, with narrow streets framed by blank walls for access. In China, courtyard houses formed almost the entire fabric of major cities such as Beijing and were, in fact, groupings of several houses serving different members of the same extended family; the houses of the wealthy typically incorporated a sequence of courtyards of increasing privacy.

Inward-looking and protective by nature, the courtyard form was antithetical to the fluid, centrifugal conception of space promoted by the first generation of Modern architects. It did, however, find favor with Mies van der Rohe: courtyardlike spaces were implicit in his Barcelona Pavilion (see pp.124–25) and he later designed several theoretical projects for houses organized around courtyards framed by an enclosing brick wall.

After 1945, partly as a result of a growing fascination with the work of ancient or distant cultures and partly as a reaction against the clamor of the modern city, courtyard forms came back into favor. In Finland, Alvar Aalto's Säynätsalo Town Hall (1949–52) offered a potent model that melded Italian civic models with memories of traditional farmyards; in Denmark, Jørn Utzon proposed courtyard house-types in a competition for the Skåne region of Sweden that later yielded his widely influential Kingo (1956–58) and Fredensborg (1959–62) housing schemes; and for the Berlin Free University (see p.55), the French practice of Candilis, Josic, and Woods built the only large-scale version of the much discussed "mat plan" that took as one of its models the Islamic city and organized the complex program of accommodation around long internal "streets" and a sequence of courtyards.

Having been rehabilitated as a spatial form, the courtyard found extended theoretical advocacy as a model for housing in 1964 with the publication of the book *Community and Privacy* by Serge Chermayeff and Christopher Alexander. Advocating houses with multiple small courtyards as a means of creating privacy between family members and offering contact with the restorative powers of nature, this was widely seen as an extreme reaction against the turbulence and diversity of modern cities. ∎

"The courtyard is by nature inward-looking and protective."

An open, arcaded coutyard, or cortile, occupied the center of most of the great Renaissance palazzi such as the Palazzo Medici in Florence shown here.

"Outdoors indoors"

ATRIUM

Derived from the Latin word used to describe the open **courtyard** at the center of the Roman house-type known as a *domus*, atrium now generally refers to a glass-covered space inside a building. Glazed atria were made possible by developments in glass technology in the nineteenth century and found particular favor for new building types such as department stores.

In Paris, for example, the world's first such, Le Bon Marché, moved into a new building (1867) designed by Louis Auguste Boileau (1812–96) and his son Louis Charles (1837–1910), which was organized around a series of glazed atria, while Galeries Lafayette acquired its celebrated art nouveau glass and steel dome in 1912.

In Scandinavia memories of the atrium's origins as a covered outdoor space were exploited by architects such as Gunnar Asplund and Alvar Aalto. Asplund's extension to the Law Courts in Gothenburg, for example, features a top-lit atrium that is linked to the open courtyard of the existing building by a glazed wall and is intended to evoke a feeling of "outdoors indoors." In Aalto's Rautatalo in Helsinki (1953–55), the offices are accessed from travertine-faced galleries that frame two sides of a space similarly envisaged as an internal piazza, replete with coffee tables below circular rooflights, the latter artificially lit from outside to melt snow and prolong the feeling of daylight within.

The ubiquity of the atrium in contemporary building has two main catalysts: the impact of the Hyatt Regency Hotel in Atlanta, completed in 1967 by the architect-developer John Portman, and the growing importance of **passive design** principles. The soaring 20-story atrium of the Hyatt Regency, complete with Portman's trademark glass "bubble" **elevators**, set the pattern for numerous hotels worldwide, culminating in the world's tallest atrium design, the Burj Al Arab in Dubai (1994–99). Similarly lofty atria have also been deployed in office buildings such as the headquarters of the HSBC in Hong Kong (1979–86, see p.92) by Foster and Partners, and in the Lloyds Building in London (1978–86, see p.167) by the Richard Rogers Partnership.

Although many atria are air conditioned and built for their value in attracting residents or tenants, their potential as part of a low-energy approach to the design of office buildings became apparent with the completion in 1983 of the Gateway Two building in Basingstoke, England. Designed by Arup Associates, it established what was to become a widely adopted approach to office design: fixed shading to prevent solar gains on the external elevations; exposed structure internally to act as a "thermal flywheel," absorbing heat by day and releasing it at night; and a glazed central atrium that, with the external glazing, provides sufficient daylight to eliminate the need for artificial lighting in the summer and drives a "stack effect" that enables stale warm air to rise and be exhausted, while drawing in fresh air from the perimeter. The savings in both capital and running costs were considerable, and Gateway Two was to be widely emulated in temperate climates. ■

An open atrium formed the focus of many ancient Roman houses, as seen here in a rare survival, the House of the Silver Wedding in Pompeii.

Glass-covered atria—seen here on the grand scale at Rafael Viñoly's Tokyo International Forum—offer numerous environmental and energy-saving advantages and have become common in offices, hotels, and many other buildings since the 1980s.

"Elevated above their surroundings, buildings assume symbolic importance."

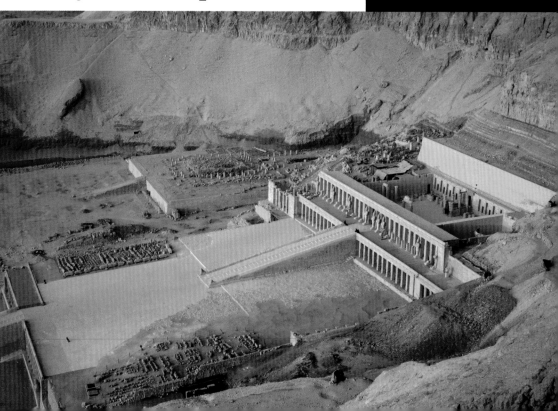

The elevated building

IDEA № 16
PLATFORM

The idea of placing buildings on raised platforms was widespread in ancient and vernacular cultures and prompted by various motives. In modern buildings platforms have often been used to house secondary spaces or services.

Practically, earth platforms frequently formed part of defensive systems, and also served to lift buildings, especially those which were of vulnerable wooden construction, above moisture and flood. Elevated above their surroundings, buildings assumed symbolic importance—hence the frequency with which temples and mortuary sites were placed on platforms. And finally, square mounds appear to have been widely seen as symbols of the supposedly flat, four-cornered Earth.

Earth mounds were subsequently made more permanent in stone. In ancient Egypt some of the grandest platforms ever built formed part of the mortuary complex of Queen Hatshepsut (opposite bottom) at Deir el-Bahri, where a colonnaded structure is reached via vast terraces. In Classical Greek architecture, the platform was stylized as a relatively shallow, three-stepped platform or stylobate; in Chinese temple complexes immense masonry structures were built to support the wooden architecture; and in several of the major Mayan sites, the temples themselves are diminutive by comparison with the massive, stepped platforms they surmount.

In 1949 the Mayan platforms were visited by a young Danish architect named Jørn Utzon. Impressed by the dramatic transition they offered from the claustrophobia of the jungle to the sensation of infinite space above the treetops, it occurred to him that something similar could be replicated in the design of contemporary buildings by housing all the secondary functions in a hollow platform and celebrating the public activities in "temples" above. It was, in essence, a large-scale version of the **servant and served** division formulated by Louis Kahn a few years later, and Utzon himself deployed it in 1957 in the design that won the competition for Sydney Opera House. The "temples" were formed by the gleaming tiled shells, while the great stepped platform —which quickly became a hugely popular public space—assumed a distinctly geological character. Echoing the headlands that jut into Sydney Harbour, it is faceted in plan and clad with precast concrete panels that incorporate the local red sandstone as an aggregate.

Given its power in helping to organize a complex building program, it is perhaps surprising that the idea of the inhabited platform has not been more widely emulated. The Welsh National Assembly, completed in 2005 to designs by Richard Rogers and Partners, echoes it on a small scale; Foreign Office Architects' Yokohama International Ferry Terminal (1995–2002, see p.184) is an inhabited platform without superstructures; and the Snøhetta-designed opera house in Oslo (2000–08, opposite top) combines Utzon's model with the idea of the **architectural promenade** as developed by Rem Koolhaas.

Seen more broadly, however, the platform can be regarded as an expression of the *piano rustica* or "rustic floor" that houses minor and service rooms in many Classical buildings and acts as the formal and functional preparation for the *piano nobile* above—an organization echoed in Le Corbusier's "**Five Points of a New Architecture**," in which the massive solidity of the *piano rustica* is replaced by an open space devoted to the flow of people and vehicles. ∎

On its completion in 1902, Otto Wagner's Post Office Savings Bank in Vienna was among the most "modern" buildings in Europe, but in planning the central banking hall Wagner turned to an ancient building type, the aisled basilica.

IDEA № 17

BASILICA

Familiar throughout the Roman Empire, the basilica was a focus of political power and place of public gathering that, rather like a medieval market hall, could function as law court, drill hall, or meeting house. It later became the archetypal form of the Christian church and the preeminent building type of European architecture.

Shortly after converting to Christianity the Roman emperor Constantine issued, in 313 AD, the Edict of Milan. This initiated a large-scale building program to create places of Christian worship throughout the empire. Until then Christians gathered, often in secret, in private homes with meeting rooms attached and so there were no architectural precedents for a purpose-built church. Adapting Roman temples was clearly out of the question—apart from the obvious difficulties inherent in taking over places devoted to pagan sacrifice, Christian services required a space for large numbers to gather in, not an imposing backdrop to outdoor ceremonies. It was decided to base the new churches on a secular Roman building-type, the basilica.

Spatially, basilicas consisted of a central hall flanked by narrower aisles that were generally lower than the nave, allowing windows to be placed between them, creating the so-called clerestory; most also had a semicircular apse extending out from one of the end walls to house the Law Court.

Adapting this arrangement for Christian worship was straightforward: the apse became the altar, presided over by priest rather than magistrate, and the congregation processed toward it from an entrance in the opposite (ideally west) end.

Decisive in the development of medieval church architecture was the building now known as Old St. Peter's, which was eventually lost to fire and replaced by the vast church we know today. As large as a Gothic cathedral, it was said to have been built over the tomb of St. Peter, the first bishop of Rome. To focus attention on this a transept was built across the nave, immediately in front of the apsidal end, with St. Peter's tomb under what would become known as the crossing. Moved a few bays westward, to create room for the choir, this became the basis of the Latin Cross plan used in most medieval and later churches—the correspondence with the form of Christ's cross is said to have been first pointed out around 380 by St. Gregory Nazianzen when describing the Church of the Holy Apostles in Constantinople. Old St. Peter's also featured double aisles and acquired two circular mausolea—a form that would later be adapted to create the chapter houses of monasteries and cathedrals.

As the model for the preeminent building type of European architecture, the basilica's importance can hardly be overstated. The basic spatial configuration of nave, aisles, and clerestory has also been reinterpreted for all manner of uses. It underpinned, for example, many of the great glasshouses of the nineteenth century, including Joseph Paxton's Crystal Palace; it has been adapted for numerous libraries, nowhere more grandly than in Labrouste's great reading room for the Bibliothèque Nationale in Paris; and it lurks behind such eminently secular "cathedrals" as Henrik Berlage's Stock Exchange in Amsterdam (see p.109) and Otto Wagner's Post Office Savings Bank in Vienna (left). ∎

“The model for the preeminent building type of European architecture.”

Built to designs by Donato Bramante, this circular martyrium in a narrow courtyard of the church of San Pietro in Montorio in Rome epitomized the Renaissance humanists' fascination with Classical Roman culture and ideal geometry.

Man is the measure of all things

IDEA № 18

HUMANISM

By the mid-fifteenth century the term humanism described both a general curriculum—the *studia humanitatis*—based on Classical authors, and a new world view. In architecture this led to buildings built around the proportions of the human figure and a new taste for the Classical forms of ancient Greece and Rome.

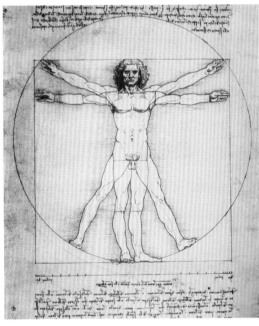

Central to the Italian Renaissance vision was the idea that the peak of human intellectual and cultural achievement was to be found in Classical Greece and Rome, knowledge of which had largely been lost following the Fall of Rome to Germanic invaders in the fifth century. Many key texts— including those of Plato—had, however, been preserved in monasteries and, following the introduction of ancient Greek to Italy, finding and translating these became a preoccupation of scholars. Crucially for architecture, the rediscovered texts included Vitruvius's *Ten Books of Architecture*.

A central tenet of Renaissance humanism was the value of the individual, famously articulated by Pico della Mirandola who—in his seminal thesis *An Oration on the Dignity of Man*—argued that unlike all other forms of life, man had been created without a fixed place "in the order of things," but had the freedom to choose either to "degenerate into the lower orders of life" or "to be born into the higher forms, which are divine." The great Craftsman, he said, had created man to contemplate His work, "to love its beauty, and to wonder at its vastness." In place of the medieval conception of architecture as the embodiment of a vision of a higher divine world, Renaissance Classicism made man "the measure of all things."

The foundations of the modern understanding of the Renaissance were established in 1860 with the publication of *The Civilization of the Renaissance in Italy* by the Swiss art historian Jacob Burckhardt (1818–97). Burckhardt stressed—many would now say overstressed—the importance of the cult of individuality that bequeathed to us the idea of artistic "genius" and an emphasis on human subjectivity: "man becomes a self-aware individual," he wrote, "and recognizes himself as such." Key exponents of this new sense of individuality were the tyrant rulers of Italy's many city-states who were determined to make their mark through conquest or the patronage of the arts—or frequently both. Complementing this subjectivity, Burckhardt pointed out that there was also awakened in Italy "an objective perception and treatment of the state and all things of this world in general."

In architecture the new sense of objectivity was manifested in the emphasis on abstract **form** and **proportion**, through which it was believed works of art could be made to conform to the principles underlying both man and the universe, while the feeling of subjectivity could be embodied using **perspective**. At first, the technique of perspective projection was seen as a means of representing accurately the supposedly objective **ideal** proportions, but it was soon realized that the two were incompatible. This opened the way to the Mannerist fascination with distortion and, ultimately, to both the Modernist espousal of the subjectivity of multiple viewpoints and the **Postmodern** rejection of all claims to the possibility of objective knowledge in science as well as the arts. ∎

Underlying harmony

IDEA Nº 19

PROPORTION

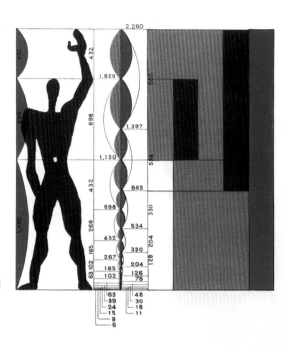

Le Corbusier's lifelong fascination with proportion as a key to architectural beauty culminated in the development of a proportioning system based on the so-called Golden Ratio, published in his book Le Modulor in 1948.

"Without symmetry and proportion there can be no principles in the design of any temple; that is, if there is no precise relation between its members as in the case of those of a well shaped man." Thus wrote Vitrivius in his *Ten Books of Architecture*, restating a belief that descends from the Pythagorean tradition of mathematics and number mysticism in Greek philosophy, but began in Mesopotamia and Egypt, where dimensions were derived from the **symmetry** and proportions of the body.

The diatonic scale in music, discovered by Pythagoras, was a major stimulus in the development of systems of proportion. Its harmonious relationships—such as an octave (1:2), fifth (3:2), and a fourth (4:3)—were seen by Pythagoras and his greatest follower, Plato, as evidence of the underlying "harmony" of nature, and a means of achieving similar qualities in works of art. They were not, however, adopted in the design of Greek temples, the dimensions of which were determined by multiples and divisions of a module determined by the column diameter at its base.

The possible systems of proportion —or so-called "sacred geometry"—used in Gothic cathedrals remain the subject of debate and seem to have derived in part from the dimensions of Solomon's Temple that were given in the Bible. Pythagorean/Platonic ideas also played a part, but it was in the Renaissance that they were overtly revived: as Alberti wrote in his *Ten Books on Architecture*, it is only natural to "borrow all our rules... for Proportions, from the Musicians."

Writing a century after Alberti, in *The Four Books of Architecture*, Andrea Palladio specified seven sets of proportions for rooms, all based on whole-number musical consonances save for one: the square and its diagonal —which, although extremely simple to draw using a pair of compasses, generated the "irrational" number 1.41414..., which many found troubling. Similarly irrational was the number produced by the most celebrated of all proportions, the "Golden Ratio." Defined as the subdivision of a line such that the ratio of the smaller to the larger segment is the same as that of the larger to the whole, it yields the ratio 1:1.68... and was used as the basis of the best-known recent attempt to regulate architecture by a system of geometric rather than modular relationships, Le Corbusier's Modulor. Published in 1948, its name was derived from the French *module* and *or* (gold).

A mathematically inconsistent elaboration of Platonic number mysticism, the Modulor was intended to be universally valid. Its dimensions were based on the somewhat arbitrary starting point of a modern Vitruvian man, for which Le Corbusier said he chose the hero of English detective stories "who was always six feet tall." His system generated two sets of dimensions, which he called the Red and Blue Scales, and although he used it in his own work, it was only adopted by a few of his most ardent admirers. The memorable graphic representation of the Modulor Man (above) did, however, become widely known, and stands as a powerful restatement of beliefs that have their roots in the earliest civilizations. ∎

Brunelleschi's Pazzi Chapel in Florence, composed using simple geometric shapes, exemplifies the Renaissance fascination with "ideal" form.

Shape, ideal, and essence

IDEA № 20
FORM

Louis-Etienne Boullée's monumental project for a cenotaph to Isaac Newton (1784, above) was the purest and grandest expression of his love of pure geometric form—an expression of the Enlightenment belief in the underlying rationality of the universe, a belief that also underpinned Claude-Nicolas Ledoux's Royal Saltworks at Arc-et-Senans (1784, below).

The meaning of the English word "form" is ambiguous, meaning both shape and, in a Platonic sense, idea or essence. In architecture it is associated with the concept of ideal form in Classical and Renaissance buildings, and with the practice of reflecting the means of construction in many nineteenth-century and, later, Modernist structures.

The division between the English meaning of shape and the sense of idea or essence is recognized in German by the words *Gestalt* (sensorial perception) and *Form* as the idea of something. The Platonic conception of form as an ideal known to the mind through intelligence, not the senses, was muddied by Aristotle who conceived of form as being linked to material things —an idea rejected by idealistic aesthetic theories, such as those of Immanuel Kant, which view beauty as independent of matter.

Despite their interest in the Platonic tradition, Renaissance architects generally used form as a synonym for shape or for the Pythagorean idea of ratio and proportion, while outside of German-speaking countries it was not until the twentieth century that a more complex understanding became general in architecture. This was of particular concern to Modernists who saw it as offering a means of defining that part of their work over which they held artistic control.

Interpretations of form were, however, surprisingly various. For Adolf Loos it represented a means of resisting ornament. In this he drew on the idea, associated with Gottfried Semper, that a given material contained its own potential form. This attitude was developed in the Deutsche Werkbund as a method of producing objects and buildings that were "true" to the form latent in a material—hence the later determination to work "**in the nature of materials**." To fully fledged Modernists of the 1920s, however, this emphasis on form risked formalism, the pursuit of form for its own sake: "form as goal is formalism," declared Mies van der Rohe in 1923.

Determined to resist Kant's influential separation of function from aesthetic value, Functionalist architects such as Hannes Meyer strove to negate any interest in form, thereby demonstrating their preoccupation with the social value of their work. This would echo down through the century. In the 1950s, for example, the Situationists attempted to resist capitalism by thinking of architecture as formless—Constant Nieuwenhuys' New Babylon project envisaged the city as an ever-changing ambience through which the post-revolutionary individual could wander from one leisure environment to another in search of new sensations.

For advocates of a radical, technology-based approach to architecture, like Cedric Price or various Utopian groups of the 1960s, a composed, static form was not a legitimate objective of architectural design. Price's Fun Palace project for the charismatic theatrical producer Joan Littlewood, for example, was a "support structure" capable of endless rearrangement, analogous on a small scale to the megastructural Plug-in City envisaged by Archigram's Peter Cook in 1964.

The dangers of formalism that worried early Modernists held no fears for Peter Eisenman. His early work of the 1970s, intended as a critique of Functionalism, drew on the linguistic theories of Ferdinand de Saussure. Saussure argued that in natural languages meanings were arbitrarily attached to forms, and in a series of provocative "house" projects Eisenman developed spatial compositions from "grammatical" operations applied to elements such as lines and planes, only later working out how the resulting form might be inhabited. ■

IDEA Nº 21

ORNAMENT

In traditional cultures, architecture, ornament, and construction were inseparable—as, for example, in the **Classical Orders**. The importance of ornament as an independent idea in architecture rests on its pivotal role in debates about such fraught issues as "authenticity" and "honesty" that eventually led to the infamous and widely misunderstood declaration, "**ornament is crime.**"

The slender columns and lifelike capitals of Deane and Woodward's neo-Gothic Museum of Natural History in Oxford (1855–60) rework in cast and wrought iron the ornamental forms of Gothic originally developed in stone.

Since the Renaissance, with growing access to world cultures and ancient civilizations ornament has come to be seen as a secondary element applied to a design, not something conceived as integral to it. Pattern books illustrating decorative systems and elements from around the world first appeared in the fifteenth century, and with the advent of the Industrial Revolution and machine production the proliferation of mass-produced ornament, often in faux materials, provoked a backlash. In Britain, the eclectic profusion of objects shown at the Great Exhibition of 1851 was in striking contrast to the modernity of the Crystal Palace that housed them. The contents may have entertained the public, but they horrified the leaders of the nascent design-reform movement.

It seems slightly ironic from a contemporary perspective that one of the most important embodiments of design reform was the best known of all pattern books, the *Grammar of Ornament* by Owen Jones, published in 1856 using the new chromolithographic process. Although his book featured designs from Egypt, Turkey, Sicily, and Spain, Jones began by explaining 37 "general principles in the arrangement of form and colour," several of which—such as the insistence on flatness in decorating walls—anticipated later Modernist practice. And it ended by arguing that "in the best periods of art, all ornament was based upon an observation of the principles which regulate the arrangement of form in nature"—an ideal that would be taken up directly by art nouveau and resonates with the Modernists' repeated invocation of nature as a model of functional design.

For the reformers, the abuse of ornament and decoration using faux materials was a moral issue: the architect Sir Robert Edis, for example, argued that "if you are content to teach a lie in your belongings, you can hardly wonder at petty deceits being practised in other ways."

Advocates of Modern architecture took two broad approaches to the problematic issue of ornament. They either eliminated it, believing that "pure" **space** and "true" construction were the best means to express the values of the emerging Machine Age, or they sought to devise a new, contemporary ornamental vocabulary. This was the route taken by Frank Lloyd Wright, whose Prairie Houses were arguably the first to embody a fully modern sense of space yet which, due to details such as their leaded-light windows, were seen by many as poised uneasily between the values of the old and the new century. ■

"Ornament has come to be seen as a secondary element applied to design, not integral to it."

The surface of Antonio Gaudí's Casa Batlló in Barcelona (1877) is decorated with a mosaic of broken ceramic tiles, while the forms of the swelling bays echo organic forms such as bones, appearing at once structural and ornamental.

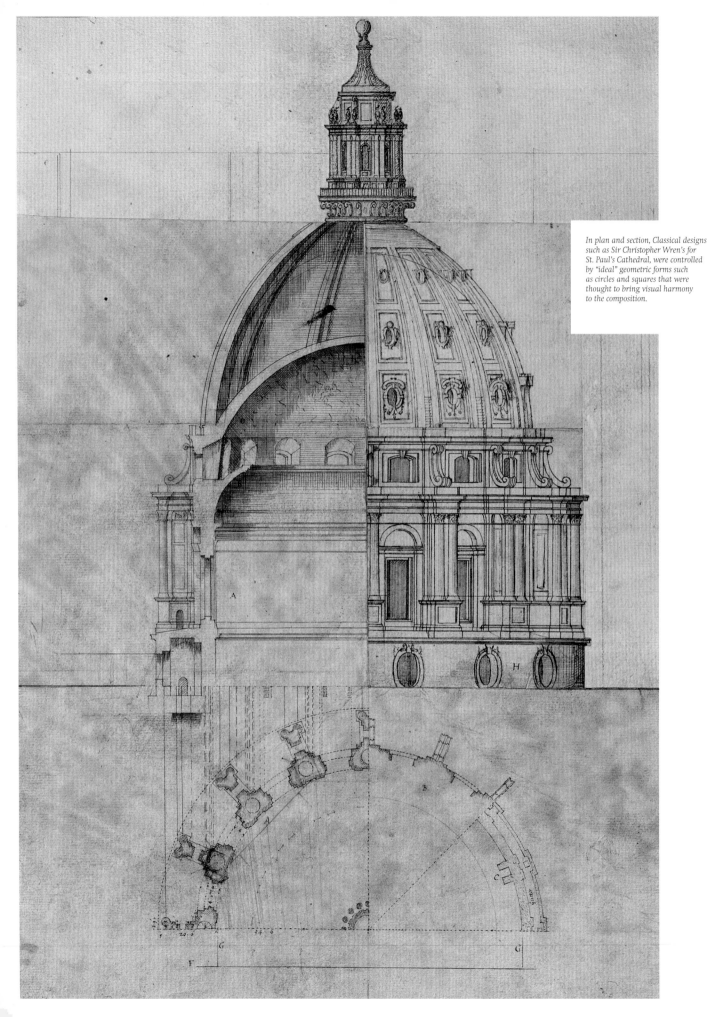

In plan and section, Classical designs such as Sir Christopher Wren's for St. Paul's Cathedral, were controlled by "ideal" geometric forms such as circles and squares that were thought to bring visual harmony to the composition.

Forms free of imperfection

IDEAL

One of the most pervasive ideas in the West is that the ultimate reality is based in the mind or ideas. In Western thought, and indeed in architecture, this has led to an attempt to represent things in an ideal form, as they ought to be rather than as they are.

Writing in *Vers une architecture* in 1923, Le Corbusier argued that by following the "Engineer's Aesthetic" the architect could achieve a "platonic grandeur" that would resonate on a "sounding-board" possessed by everyone. This universal aesthetic for the Machine Age was inspired by the "law of economy" and governed by "mathematical calculation."

This "idealist" view derives from Plato, and its interpretation continues to exercise philosophers. The primary impact on architecture, however, is easier to describe. By arguing that all objects in the physical realm are imperfect variations of ideal versions that exist in the realm of ideas Plato gave rise to a tradition of representation of the ideal form. This inspired recurring visions of **Utopia** and conditioned the Classical view of architecture, one of the clearest summaries of which was given by Sir Christopher Wren (1632–1723):

> There are two causes of beauty – natural and customary. Natural is from geometry consisting in uniformity, that is equality and proportion. Customary beauty is begotten by the use, as familiarity breeds a love for things not in themselves lovely. Here lies the great occasion of errors, but always the true test is natural or geometrical beauty. Geometrical figures are naturally more beautiful than irregular ones: the square, the circle are the most beautiful, next the parallelogram and the oval. There are only two beautiful positions of straight lines, perpendicular and horizontal; this

is from Nature and consequently necessity, no other than upright being firm.

This attitude pervades the emphasis on **form**, **proportion**, and **symmetry** in the earlier treatises of Alberti and Palladio, and was pursued with renewed vigor in Neoclassical theory and practice under the influence of the art historian Johann Joachim Winckelmann (1717–68).

Espousing the "noble simplicity and quiet grandeur" of Greek sculpture, Winckelmann rejected the sensual nature of art and advocated an idealized expressionless beauty based on "pure" form, free of such "secondary" properties as color and texture—much as Le Corbusier would later advocate the "Law of Ripolin" (a French whitewash) as a means of revealing the formal qualities of architecture that appealed to the mind rather than merely gratified the senses.

In an influential essay published in 1947 under the title "The Mathematics of the Ideal Villa," Colin Rowe compared Le Corbusier's early work with that of Palladio. In his buildings, as opposed to his polemically simplified theories, we see a continual dialog between what can be interpreted as an "ideal" system of order—the column **grid**, for example—and the specific demands of program, site, or construction. In a similar way, reflecting his **Beaux-Arts** education with its emphasis on the parti, Louis Kahn's projects began with an idealized **Form** (his capitalization) that was tested and realized by the discipline of Design. ∎

Designed for the 1979 Venice Biennale, Aldo Rossi's Teatro del Mondo exemplified his belief that ideal geometric forms had the power to embody the cultural "memory" of the city.

Standard unit for assembling space and form

IDEA Nº 23
MODULE

The dimensions of a Greek temple were coordinated by using multiples or fractions of half the diameter of the columns at its base—an early example of a dimensional module in architecture.

From Japanese houses laid out according to the standard size of tatami mats to the banal repetition of suspended ceiling tiles, the use of repeated modules is encountered throughout architecture.

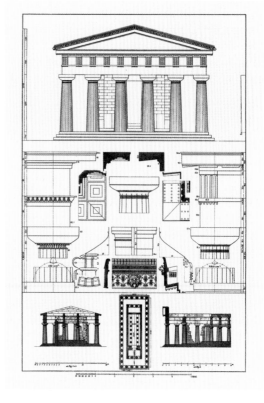

The ancient Greeks adopted such a system in proportioning the **Classical Orders**: the chosen module was half the diameter of the column measured at its base, divided into 30 equal parts. In the same spirit, in his celebrated *Ten Books of Architecture*, the Roman architect Vitruvius advised that "within a temple a certain part should be selected as a standard... the size of the module for Doric temples should equal the width of a triglyph."

The extent to which such systems determined every dimension of a Greek temple is open to debate, whereas in Chinese wood-framing systems, documented in construction manuals such as the *Yingzao fashi* (1103) and *Gongcheng zuofa zeli* (1733), the use of standardized modules to control the construction details and layout of buildings was determined by imperial edict. Published as government construction regulations applicable throughout the empire these manuals had much the same ambition as modern efforts to develop internationally coordinated systems of dimensions and components.

In European architecture the shift from geometric systems of proportion, believed to attune buildings to the cosmos and the human body, to the "rational" requirements of industrial construction became explicit in the work of the French architect and teacher Jean-Nicolas-Louis Durand (1760–1834). In two influential books summarizing his teaching, generally abbreviated as *Le Recueil* and *Le Précis*

(the full titles being exceedingly long), Durand laid down methods familiar to architecture students today. *Le Recueil* offered 92 "precedent studies" to facilitate analysis and emulation of historic buildings with the same functional program, while the latter dealt with "modern" needs—hygiene and health, administration and justice, education and politics. The *Précis* culminated through several editions in an abstract compositional method based on intersecting axes and grids, coordinated by gridded paper to which modular elements of "architecture" were added.

Durand's pragmatic approach anticipated later attempts to systematize both architectural knowledge—most famously, perhaps, by Ernst Neufert (1900–86), whose book *Architects' Data*, first published in 1936, was widely translated and emulated—and the assembly and dimensional coordination of industrially produced components. The latter also began in France, in the work of the army engineer Colonel Charles Renard who, in the 1870s, proposed preferred numbers for use with the metric system, which were eventually adopted in 1952 by the International Organization for Standardization as ISO3. Renard's geometric and logarithmic sequences were considered too complex for construction, where a "basic module" of 100mm was chosen, with multiples of 300mm, 600mm, and 1200mm successively to be favored as dimensions increased in size.

Although essentially pragmatically motivated in most contemporary buildings, modularity has inspired numerous architects toward a more poetic vision: from Jean Prouvé's pioneering efforts to develop industrialized building systems via Moshe Safdie's Habitat housing at the 1968 Montreal Expo to the contemporary fascination with computer-generated systems, the potential pleasures of modular repetition have been a recurring theme of modern architecture. ∎

RIGHT: *This British CLASP school, built using a system of modular components, won a prize at the Venice Biennale in 1960.*

"Modularity has inspired numerous architects toward a more poetic vision."

BELOW: *Traditional Japanese houses were laid out using standard, body-sized tatami mats as a planning module.*

"A modular grid was meant to be both rational and universally applicable."

The Jefferson Grid, which divided the American landscape into 1-mile (1.6-km) squares of 640 acres (259 ha), was introduced to facilitate the colonization of the western states. As seen in this aerial view of Chicago, it still permeates American cities and landscapes.

IDEA № 24

GRID

The use of a square or rectangular grid of crossing, parallel lines to organize space began at the scale of town planning in several ancient civilizations from the Americas to China. It is probably best known from what is thought to be the first grid-planned Greek town: Miletus; commonly— albeit with scant evidence—attributed to Hippodamus (c.500–440 BC), its plan was the first to articulate the value of the grid as an expression of social order and rationality.

The grid planning of Roman towns derived from military camps and was organized around two principal streets, set at right angles to each other and called the *cardo*—which ran north– south—and the *decumanus*. As the empire expanded, this geographical system was extended across Europe as a means of imposing order on occupied territory, anticipating later large-scale systems such as the Jefferson Grid of 1-mile- (1.6-km-) square plots introduced in 1785 to extend government authority over the Mississippi River and Great Lakes regions, but eventually expanded across much of the United States.

In architecture, the first concerted attempt to promote the use of an abstract grid of dimensions to co- ordinate the plans, sections, and elevations of buildings was made in France by the influential **Beaux-Arts** teacher Jean-Nicolas-Louis Durand (1760–1834). Advocating an egalitarian post-Revolutionary architecture, he used the new "basic architectural meter" as a module. This was measured as the center-to-center distance between columns, rather than—as in Classical practice—as a column diameter, which had been proportionally related to the human body since antiquity.

Like "The Rights of Man," Durand's architecture, built on a modular grid, was meant to be both rational and universally applicable. It proved popular in Germany, where it was adopted by leading Neoclassicists such as Karl Friedrich Schinkel (1781–1841) and Leo von Klenze (1784–1864), and it is no coincidence that the first attempt to provide comprehensive dimensional guidance for architects was made there a century later, by Ernst Neufert (see p.52), a former assistant of Walter Gropius at the Bauhaus.

The perceived universality and rationality of the grid held an obvious appeal for architects seeking an **International Style** for the Machine Age, and grids are widely used as both abstract compositional devices and a means of coordinating the dimensions of a building and the components with which it is built—increasingly important in a globalized economy in which buildings are assembled from factory-produced components that allow little or no room for adjustment on-site.

With the development of the Modernist **free plan**, the structural grid became the means of allowing unprecedented freedom in the organization of space, whereas in the work of an architect like OM Ungers (left bottom), the systematic gridding of space is used as a means of imposing an unyielding order on everything from the dimensions of rooms and furniture to the location of electrical sockets and light switches. In their adoption of the grid, however, both these otherwise opposed attitudes belong to the Modern discourse of universal **space** rather than the **Postmodern** concern with the particularities of **place**. ∎

Perfect balance

IDEA № 25
SYMMETRY

In common usage "symmetry" connotes specifically that preference for bilaterial symmetry around a central axis that is found in the formal architectures of all civilizations and widely in vernacular buildings. This seems to be so universal and deeply ingrained that its origins are almost certainly biological.

As well as sharing the use of axial symmetry in their spatial organization, the decoration of Islamic buildings abounds in complex forms of symmetry rarely encountered in Western architecture.

Our individuality may rest on minor facial asymmetries—hence the other-worldliness of the symmetrical representations of faces in icons—but significant departures from bodily symmetry are commonly seen as indicators of sickness or deformity. Rather than being an idea that changed architecture, therefore, symmetry might perhaps be better described as an idea that defined it in the first place by fusing bodily and cosmic symbolism.

The word "symmetry" itself is derived from the Greek *symmetria* which, in the most celebrated ancient aesthetic treatise to survive, the *Canon of Polyclitus*, was used to designate the "commensurability" of all parts of a sculpture to each other and to the whole. This idea can be traced back to a number of theories of Pythagoras and the Platonic tradition of thought and it underpins the broader understanding of symmetry in both the Western Classical and Islamic traditions.

Although bilateral symmetry is by far the most common form encountered in Western architecture, its stronger counterpart—symmetry around two axes crossing at right angles—has been frequently used in the composition of

individual rooms and, in the Renaissance, in the expression of the search for **ideal** form. In the Islamic world more complex forms of mathematical symmetry were deployed, both in the overall planning of buildings and in tiling patterns, which exhibit complex translations, rotations, and reflections (left). The resulting quasi-crystalline patterns are of such sophistication that they anticipate recent mathematical theory on symmetry and tiling.

Symmetry is one of the most effective means of asserting the importance of a work of architecture such as a church or other public building, by making it stand out from the natural environment and the contingent fabric of the city—the opposite of camouflage, in which asymmetrical markings are used to break up a readily identifiable form. Conversely, symmetry is also a means of creating rooms that, by being readily understood, may more effectively draw attention to the artifacts or events they house rather than to themselves.

The first concerted challenge to the dominance of symmetry in formal architecture came in Britain in the

eighteenth century, with the advocacy of a new aesthetic category, the **Picturesque**. Nature, in the form of landscape rather than organisms, again provided the model: Picturesque scenes—and by extension, paintings and buildings—had to be full of variety, engaging details, and rough textures, and exhibit a determined lack of symmetry. The freeing of architectural composition from the supposed tyranny of symmetry became a defining feature of the **Gothic Revival**, the Arts and Crafts movement, and of the **International Style**, where it was used as a means of achieving the spatial fluidity and formal contrasts that were seen as an expression of the dynamism of modern life. ∎

Although an avowedly modern architect, Louis Kahn embraced aspects of Classical composition including axial symmetry—as seen here at his Salk Institute Laboratories in La Jolla, California (1959–66).

IDEA № 26

COMMODITY, FIRMNESS, AND DELIGHT

"Well-building hath three conditions: commodity, firmness and delight." With these words, known as the Vitruvian triad, the author and diplomat Sir Henry Wotton created the English-language version of what has become the most commonly cited "definition" of architecture.

They appeared in his 1624 book, *The Elements of Architecture*, a free translation of the Roman architect Vitruvius's *De Architectura*, now universally known as the *Ten Books of Architecture* and the only architectural treatise to survive from classical antiquity.

Born around 80–70 BC, Vitruvius owes his fame entirely to his "Ten Books." In the original Latin, the Vitruvian triad was *firmitas*, *utilitas*, and *venustas*—meaning that a work of architecture must be strong or durable, useful, and beautiful. Following ideas in Greek and Roman aesthetic theory, Vitruvius saw architecture as an imitation of nature. Just as birds and bees build nests, so humans construct housing from natural materials to shelter them against the elements. This quasi-natural art of building was perfected in ancient Greece with the invention of the **Classical Orders** that instilled a sense of proportion—the source of *venustas* or beauty—and led them to understand the greatest of all forms, the human body.

To illustrate his ideal of beauty as being grounded in the proportions of the human body, Vitruvius presented the figure of a man, later made famous by Leonardo da Vinci, shown with legs and arms outstretched and neatly inscribed in a circle and a square (see p.43), "**ideal**" shapes that represented the cosmic order, and were governed by the Golden Ratio.

Vitruvius's books were rediscovered in Renaissance Italy and radically reformulated by Leon Battista Alberti in his widely influential *De Re Aedificatoria*: written between 1443–52 but not published until 1485, it has been described as the "most important work of architectural theory ever written." Although he set out to replace Vitruvius's authority, Alberti's book adopted the Vitruvian model and discussed the work of the architect according to the categories of solidity, use, and grace. His Latin and his ideas were more precise than his predecessor's, and more than anyone else it was Alberti who established architecture as a profession underpinned by intellectual theory rather than craft practice.

Despite Alberti's desire to distance himself from Vitruvius, they shared the view that beauty was an inherent quality of a work of art, not something added, and that in architecture it was not merely a by-product of paying due attention to commodity and firmness alone, as hard-line advocates of "form follows function"—such as the German Functionalist Hannes Meyer—would eventually maintain. As Le Corbusier, a latter-day Vitruvian at heart, famously wrote in his 1923 book *Vers une architecture* (translated into English as *Towards a New Architecture*): "You employ stone, wood, and concrete, and with these materials you build houses and palaces: that is construction. Ingenuity is at work. But suddenly you touch my heart, you do me good. I am happy and I say: This is beautiful. That is Architecture." ∎

The Greek Doric order, frequently compared to the proportions of a man and said to be "swelling" under the imposed load (far left), epitomizes the integration of structure ("firmness") and visual pleasure ("delight"). The Doric temples at Paestum in southern Italy (left) feature the most generous swelling —entasis—of any surviving ancient Greek buildings and were much admired by Neoclassical architects.

Leon Battista Alberti's Church of
Sant' Andrea in Mantua, designed
c.1470, exemplifies the Renaissance
revival of the Vitruvian triad into
an aesthetic whole.

Responding to purpose, locale, and materials

IDEA № 27

PARTICULARITY

In philosophy, the word "particulars" is used to describe concrete things existing in space and time, which stand in opposition to **abstractions**. The word "particular" may not come to mind as readily as ideas infused with the Platonic world view—**form**, **ideal**, **symmetry**, **proportion**—but it describes recurring attitudes in architecture, from responding to the **genius loci** and a concern for **place** rather than **space**, to designing **in the nature of materials**.

The Classical idealization of form was widely rejected by Gothic masons in favor of an interest in the particular qualities of things: nowhere was this more apparent than in their representation of recognizable species of leaves, as seen here at Southwell Minster, Nottinghamshire, England.

The Classical view to which a concern with the particular is frequently opposed was admirably presented by the painter Sir Joshua Reynolds in his *Discourses on Art*. The power of art, he declared, lay in discovering, in order to eliminate, "what is particular and uncommon" so that art could "rise above all singular forms, local customs, particularities and details of every kind." Against this, his contemporary and adversary, the poet William Blake, declared that "art and science cannot exist but in minutely organized particulars."

In architecture, the fascination with the particular blossomed in the Gothic cathedrals, where the Platonic framework of the building became a foil to naturalistic detail. Thanks to an influential essay by Nikolaus Pevsner the exquisitely carved oak leaves in the chapter house at Southwell Minster (right) in England have been seen as a key turning point, but diverse species of plants were also faithfully captured at Chartres and other cathedrals in the Ile-de-France.

The importance of looking at nature in this way can hardly be overstated. From it stems the empirical spirit of modern science and the attitude to art that gave us the English landscape garden, with its concern for **Picturesque** delights. It also underpins the attitude to materials that embraces both their engineering properties and the desire to express their "nature" that played such a fundamental role in the development of Modern architecture.

Few buildings better illustrate both these aspects than Frank Lloyd's Fallingwater (1935, opposite). From the overall composition to the facture of its walls, stairs, windows, and other details, its stratification echoes the sedimentary geology of the site; approaching the entrance under a concrete trellis you notice that one beam has been made to curve around a tree, celebrating both its particular presence and the attitude to nature embodied in the architecture; and finally the handling of materials is calculated to express their individual "nature"—the cantilevered balconies, for example, are a dramatic expression of the structural potential of **reinforced concrete**, while their rounded corners reflect Wright's belief that reinforced concrete was essentially a liquid material.

In architecture the particular generally exists in counterpoint to the generic. Characterizing such a synthesis as "the difficult whole," American architect Robert Venturi described a host of examples and design tactics in his 1966 book *Complexity and Contradiction in Architecture*. In Le Corbusier's unmistakeably **"ideal"** Villa Savoye (see p.141), for example, the clarity of the parti is brought alive by responding to a succession of particular requirements, from the broad sweep of the turning curve of a car that determines the geometry of the glazed screen at ground-floor level, to the way a partition is wrapped around a bath. ∎

"I follow in building the principles that nature has used in its domain."
—*Frank Lloyd Wright*

Frank Lloyd Wright's determination to design houses in response to the particular qualities of a site is seen as its most spectacular in Fallingwater (1935) where everything from the overall "geological" stratification to a concrete trellis wrapped around a tree trunk reflects this aspiration.

"An embattled artist-hero struggling to create civilization's greatest achievements."

Emergence of the artist-hero

IDEA № 28
ARCHITECT

As its derivation from the Greek words for "chief" and "carpenter" suggests, the term "architect" is ancient. The current idea of the architect as an independent professional knowledgeable in all aspects of design and construction, however, has more recent roots in the Renaissance and was consolidated only in the eighteenth century.

The role of "master builder" persisted into the Middle Ages, undergoing a significant shift with the emergence of Gothic architecture in France in the twelfth century. Rather than seeing buildings organically, and allowing them to grow and change, the Gothic master masons were skilled in geometry and able not only to delineate complex stone forms, but also to give a unifying spatial/geometric structure to the whole building.

With the revival of Classical learning in the Renaissance, and the rediscovery of Vitruvius's treatise on architecture, the view of the architect as a quasi-artist skilled in both the art of composition and the practicalities of building—in other words, a designer—began to develop. Many of the great Renaissance and Baroque figures—Michelangelo, Leonardo, Raphael, Bernini—moved freely between the various visual arts and a vital, if surprising, key to the new role of architect was the widespread availability of adequate-sized sheets of paper, without which the drawing of designs would have been impossible.

The Renaissance conception of architecture as an art initiated a growing separation between design and the practical craft of building. The advancement of the latter increasingly fell to another new profession, that of engineer, and the separation between the two was institutionalized in France in the seventeenth century with the foundation of the Ecole des Beaux-arts, which taught architecture, and of the Ecole Nationale des Ponts et Chaussées, which trained what we would now call civil engineers.

The romantic idea of the architect as an embattled artist-hero struggling to create civilization's greatest achievements originated with writers such as Goethe, who was in awe of the beauty of Gothic cathedrals, and was adopted by architects such as Le Corbusier and Frank Lloyd Wright. The latest reinvention of this role is the "starchitect," a designer able to put cities and clients "on the map" and a recognizable marketing tool: the architect of modern advertising dresses in black, wears spectacles, and a bow tie, and carries a roll of drawings—and has been used to sell watches and shoes, fashion, and furniture.

The reality of modern practice, for most architects, is very different. Some work as architect-entrepreneurs, a role previously banned by many professional codes of conduct but pioneered in the U.S. since the 1950s by the likes of John Portman; some as community advocates; and many more in large corporate firms and **design and build** contractors, where increasingly the process of design is broken down into specialized tasks. This trajectory recalls Karl Marx's analysis of factory work, that it divides holistic tasks previously undertaken by skilled craftsmen into specialized partial skills—a long way from the master builder or artist-hero of popular mythology. ∎

In the Middle Ages the design and building processes were both under the direction of a master mason, who rose through a system of craft apprenticeship.

The three-dimensional building described in two dimensions

IDEA № 29

ORTHOGRAPHIC PROJECTION

Representing buildings using coordinated scale plans, sections, and elevations, and the drawing boards and T squares or parallel motions that facilitated their production, are very familiar but orthographic projections did not come into general use until the nineteenth century.

Plans are ancient, some dating to the third millennium BC, and a sectional drawing of Rheims Cathedral is found in the celebrated sketchbook of Villard de Honnecourt, made in the early thirteenth century. But the systematic use of orthography, which enables the designer to produce two-dimensional drawings that completely describe the three-dimensional form of a building, stems from the development of descriptive geometry by Gaspard Monge in the late eighteenth century.

The first known coordinated plan and section drawings date from 1390, but they were made as a study of Milan Cathedral by Antonio di Vincenzo, who had just been awarded the commission for San Petronio in Bologna, not to guide its construction—which, as was usual, had begun without a fixed idea of its sectional form. Although full-size drawings were used to guide intricate work on Gothic buildings, it was only in the Renaissance that scale drawings came into widespread use. The use of scale promoted an intellectual separation between drawing and building, and with it the emergence of the separate roles of architect and craftsman.

The most obvious immediate impact of drawings was in the tendency of some Early Renaissance buildings, such as Alberti's Palazzo Rucellai (see p.12), to resemble incised drawings: the "architecture" of its elevation was in effect a stone **cladding** laid over the actual construction. Philosophically,

the new importance of drawing reflected the belief that visual observation, not just divine revelation, could be the primary source of knowledge, while pragmatically it was made possible by developments in paper-making, developing in parallel with artists' use of extensive drawn studies for paintings.

Making scale drawings encouraged architects to think of architecture in the terms that drawings best described, that is to say as problems of three-dimensional/spatial **form**. This emphasis on formal problems, and the temptation—epitomized by the grandiose projects fostered by the Ecole des Beaux-arts in Paris—to treat drawings as ends in themselves, led Le Corbusier to advise students to "develop a loathing for drawings" that were no more than "shimmering displays" of graphic skill. Equally, the use of plans, sections, and elevations as generators of form had no more vigorous defender: in *Vers une architecture* Le Corbusier explained that the "austere abstraction" of the plan was the "decisive moment" in the creation of architecture and extolled the virtue of "regulating lines" in determining the **proportions** of an elevation.

Le Corbusier's early villas, combined with the work of the Italian Modernist Giuseppe Terragni, were catalysts for arguably the most radical attempt of all, by Peter Eisenman, to use the mechanisms of projective

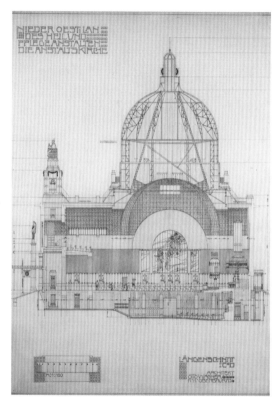

drawing as the means of generating architectural form. In a series of "House" projects produced in the 1970s, Eisenman subjected abstract elements—lines, planes, grids, etc—to transformations that anticipated the **computer-aided design** software packages that many believe will replace orthographic drawing as the primary means of generating and representing architecture. ∎

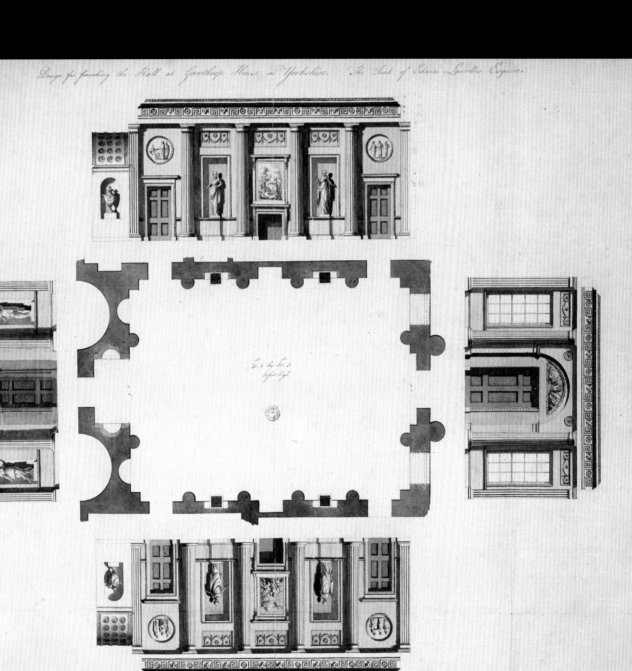

Representing space and view

LEFT: *Completed in 1901, Frank Lloyd Wright's Ward Willits House is generally regarded as the first of his influential Prairie Houses. Like most of Wright's perspectives, this drawing was almost certainly made for publication after the house was built.*

OPPOSITE: *This beautiful watercolor rendering of the project for Otto Wagner's own house in Vienna was published in 1890 in the first of a four-part edition of his work. As can be seen from the construction lines on the plan, the center of projection for the perspective lies just off the sheet.*

IDEA Nº 30
PERSPECTIVE PROJECTION

Invented as a technique to represent the world as we supposedly perceive it, perspective projection became both a means of design and the catalyst for far-reaching doubts that questioned the foundations of Classical architecture.

The story of Filippo Brunelleschi's discovery—or rediscovery—of linear perspective is among the best known in art history. Invited to peer through a conical hole in the door of Florence Cathedral, people saw, reflected in a mirror, a painting he had made of the Baptistery; swiftly removing the mirror Brunelleschi revealed the actual view, which appeared magically similar to the painting.

The ideas on which perspective projection was based were ancient—Euclid's *Optica* defined the visual ray and cone around 300 BC, while Vitruvius tantalizingly observed that "perspective is the method of sketching a front with the sides withdrawing into the background, the lines all meeting in the centre of a circle"—but its implications proved radically modern. Following the art historian Erwin Panofsky, many see the unified visual field that perspective projection assumes as the beginnings of the view of space as an infinite continuum rationalized by Descartes and Kant and embraced by Modernist architects.

Beyond painting, the earliest applications of perspective—as in ancient Greece and Rome—were in the theater. The Teatro Olimpico in Vicenza (see p.83), designed by Palladio and completed by Vincenzo Scamozzi in 1584, remains the most celebrated example thanks to the survival of Scamozzi's original sets: lit from within, they create an almost perfect illusion of "real" streets—perfect, that is, if you are sitting at the center of projection. The one-point perspective stage set, projected from the sovereign's seat in the royal box, was brought to a peak by Giacomo Torelli (1608–78) at the court of Louis XIV of France. Many of his stages appeared to extend to infinity. Similar techniques were deployed by André le Nôtre in the design of perspectival illusions in the gardens of Versailles.

As the love of perspective spread like wildfire in the theater, or as a means of extending the apparent space of Baroque interiors by using vast wall or ceiling paintings, in architecture they precipitated a crisis that cut to the core of Renaissance theory: if beauty lay in mathematically "correct" **proportions**, like those governing musical harmony, how could they be apprehended if, to the eye, they appeared distorted? While few architects now share the Classical belief in **ideal** proportions, many question the value of perspective projections, so easily generated by **CAD** modeling software, as a vehicle for *designing*—in the manner of the **Picturesque**—rather than *representing* a building. Frank Lloyd Wright was adamant about this: writing in 1908 he argued "No man ever built a building worthy the name of architecture who fashioned it in perspective sketch to his taste and then fudged the plan to suit. Such methods produce mere scene-painting. A perspective may be a proof, but it is no nurture." More recently, drawing on **phenomenology**, theorists such as Juhani Pallasmaa have implicated perspective projection in the overemphasis on the visual rather than tactile, acoustic, and other aspects of an embodied architectural experience. ∎

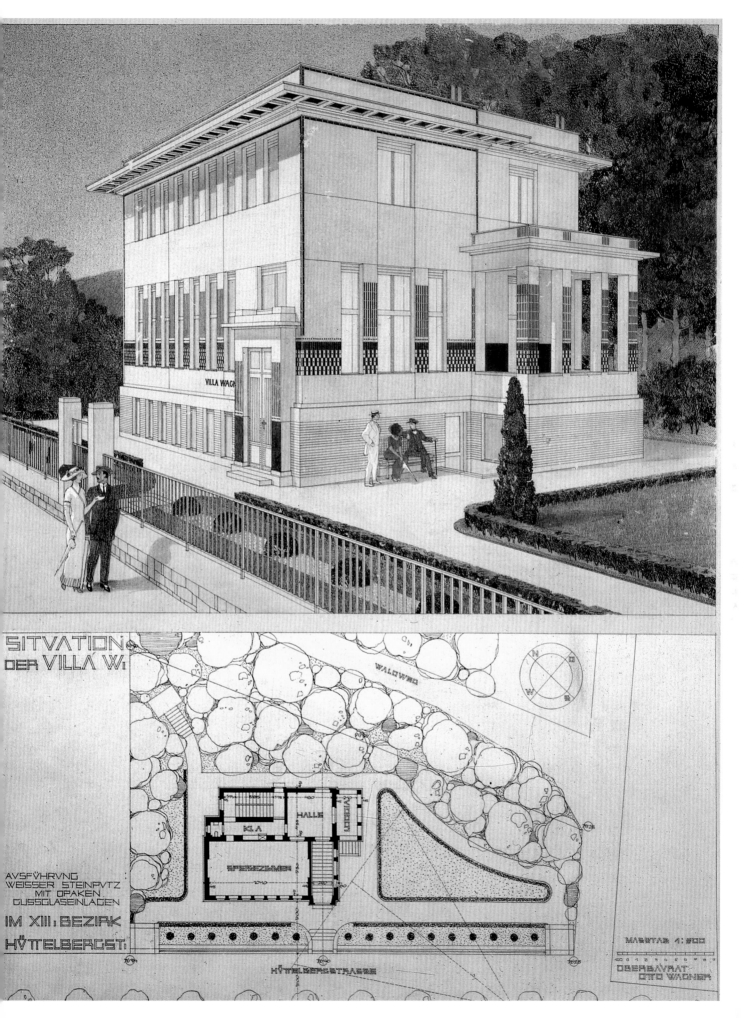

VILLA WAGN

SITVATION
DER VILLA W:

WALDWEG

N

O

W

S

AVSFÜHRVNG
WEISSER STEINPVTZ
MIT OPAKEN
GVSSGLASEINLAGEN

IM XIII. BEZIRK
HÜTTELBERGSTR.

KL.A   HALLE

SPEISEZIMMER

MASSTAB 1: 200

OBERBAVRAT
OTTO WAGNER

HÜTTELBERGSTRASSE

Alberti's design for the façade of Santa Maria Novella in Florence, completed in 1470, was composed using an underlying geometry of squares, circles, and their regular subdivisions.

The art of arrangement

COMPOSITION

The term "composition" is derived from the Latin words meaning "to put together," and at various times has been all but interchangeable with such related ideas as design, form, visual order, or formal structure.

Due to its more extensive use in the other visual arts and in music, the term has tended to be favored by writers or practitioners keen to associate architecture with other forms of art, whereas those who used analogies with machines or natural **organisms**, preferred to speak of architectural organization—hence Le Corbusier's advice to students: "architecture is organization. You are an organizer, not a drawing-board artist."

Any composition involves an explicit or implicit system of rules governing the arrangement of elements. The earliest was probably **proportion**, which can be traced back to Greek mathematics and found its first application in music. This and related ideas were eventually distilled into number systems—for example by Fibonacci—and led, in the Renaissance, to systems of composition based on numbers and formal rules such as **symmetry** that governed, for example, the "ideal" villas of Palladio (see p.75).

Arguably the most systematic approach to architectural composition was developed under the French Beaux-Arts system (see pp.88–89) and disseminated by Jean-Nicolas-Louis Durand (1760–1834), who taught at the Ecole Nationale Polytechnique. His first book, *Réceuil et parallèle des édifices en tout genre, anciens et modernes* (1799–1801), published plans of numerous buildings at the same scale, for the purposes of analysis in what would now be called "precedent studies," while his second, *Précis des leçons d'architecture données à l'Ecole Polytechnique* (1802–05), explained systematic methods for both analyzing and composing buildings. Durand's method used elemental geometric figures to generate volumetric designs: complexity was achieved by an additive process, working from part to whole, rather than through proportional regulation of the whole.

Although "organization" was widely preferred to "composition" by functionally inclined Modernists, the term has recently come back into favor. In *Complexity and Contradiction in Architecture* (1966) Robert Venturi offered a repertoire of compositional techniques derived—rather like Durand, albeit in a much less systematic way—from the study of precedents. Similarly, in his book *Architectural Composition* (1988), Rob Krier revived a more holistic, Classically based approach by bringing together ideas on elements, form, proportion, function, and construction.

At the other end of the spectrum from Venturi and Krier, who ground their ideas in history, is the recent return to number-based approaches to composition that exploit the computational power of digital computers. These frequently allude to the mathematical ideas developed by the so-called **Postmodern** "sciences of complexity," such as chaos theory and fractal geometries, and echo, albeit with very different formal consequences, the belief of Greek and Renaissance theorists that nature can be understood through number. Popularized through books such as Charles Jencks' *The Architecture of the Jumping Universe* (1995), who sees them echoed in the work of Frank Gehry,

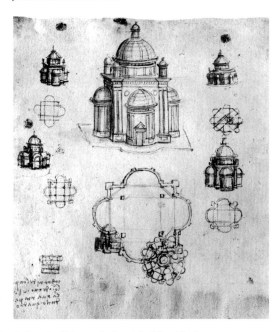

Leonardo da Vinci's sketches for a centrally planned church, c.1492, illustrate a compositional form—a circle with multiple cross axes—that fascinated Renaissance architects.

Zaha Hadid, and Daniel Libeskind, among others, these ideas have found a potent advocate in the work of the engineer Cecil Balmond, who combines mathematical brilliance with a fertile structural and spatial imagination. ■

The ideal place

Traditionally attributed to Piero della Francesca this view of an Ideal City (c.1470) is now thought to be by Leon Battista Alberti, projecting a view of the harmonious Classical buildings described in his De Re Aedificatoria.

IDEA № 32
UTOPIA

Formed by combining the Greek words for "not" and "place," *Utopia*, was the title of a 1516 book by scholar and statesman Sir Thomas More (1478–1535). Modeled on Plato's *Republic*, it described a fictional island where an apparently perfect society flourished. In this sense the word "Utopia" has come to describe visions of the **"ideal"** city.

Renaissance Utopian visions had a surprising starting point: the star-shaped layout adopted by Florence to resist cannon fire. This was widely adopted, most famously by Filarete in his proposal for an ideal city named Sforzinda, published c.1464 as part of his *Treatise on Architecture*. Its 12-pointed shape, circumscribed by a circle, embodied the fifteenth-century fascination with geometry, and Filarete also offered astrological advice on how to secure celestial harmony.

The next major wave of Utopian thought developed in the nineteenth century in response to the perceived ills and potentials of industrialization. Ebenezer Howard's (1850–1928) Garden City model, published in 1898 in *To-morrow: a Peaceful Path to Real Reform* (reissued in 1902 as *Garden Cities of To-morrow*), was planned on a concentric pattern with radial boulevards (opposite)—memories of Filarete—and intended to be self-sufficient in food,

anticipating current ideas of the sustainable city.

Howard's vision was widely influential, not least on Le Corbusier. Gathered together and published as *La Ville Radieuse* (The Radiant City) in 1935, Le Corbusier's ideas about an "ideal" modern city based on tall blocks served by elevated highways and set in a continuous sea of green space were proposed as the antithesis of the ills of traditional cities overwhelmed by the impact of industrialization—which he summed up as "tubercular Paris." These ideas dominated the *Congrès International d'Architecture Moderne* (CIAM) when it met in 1933 to discuss the needs of the industrial city. Its proceedings were eventually published in 1942 by Le Corbusier in a drastically edited form in *The Athens Charter*, and exerted considerable, often damaging, influence on postwar reconstruction.

Among later Utopian visions spawned by Modernism, a recurring

theme has been the reduction of architecture to an enabling infrastructure of services. This informed the "Spatial City" (1958) of Yona Friedman; the seemingly more pragmatic, but technically Utopian, vision of housing articulated by N.J. Habraken in *Supports, an Alternative to Mass Housing*, published in 1962; and the "Continuous Monument: An Architectural Model for Total Urbanization" of the Italian group Superstudio, formed in 1966 by Adolfo Natalini and Cristiano Toraldo di Francia.

Opposition to Modernist ideas on the city have recently centered around Utopian visions based on a return to preindustrial, often Classical, urban, and architectural forms. Pioneered by Leon Krier, among others, these formed around the "new urbanism" movement that began in the U.S. in the early years of the 1980s. ■

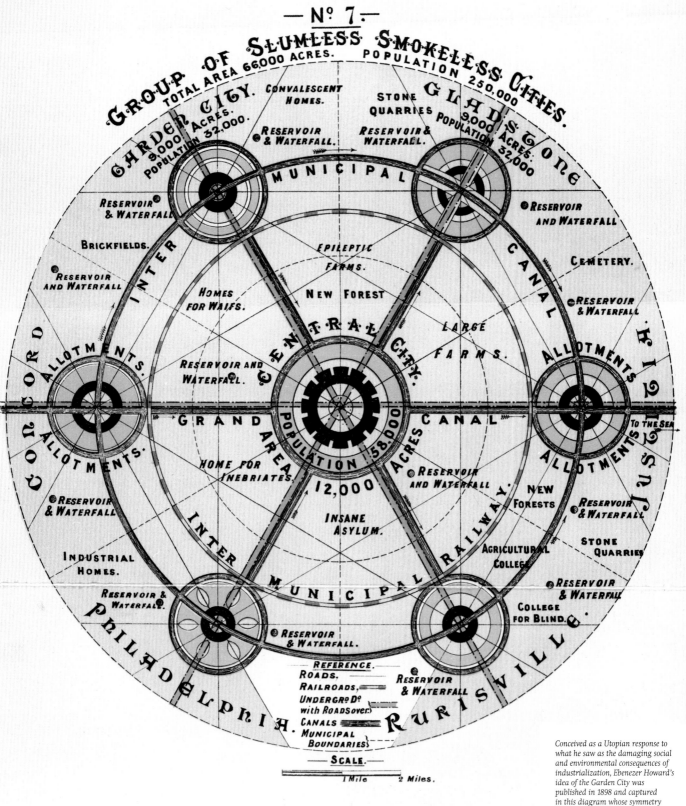

— N⁰ 7 —

GROUP·OF·SLUMLESS·SMOKELESS·CITIES.

TOTAL AREA 66000 ACRES.   POPULATION 250,000

GARDEN CITY.
9,000 ACRES.
POPULATION 32,000.

GLADSTONE
9,000 ACRES
POPULATION 32,000

CONVALESCENT HOMES.

STONE QUARRIES.

RESERVOIR & WATERFALL.

RESERVOIR & WATERFALL.

MUNICIPAL

RESERVOIR AND WATERFALL

RESERVOIR & WATERFALL

INTER

CANAL

CEMETERY.

BRICKFIELDS.

RESERVOIR AND WATERFALL

EPILEPTIC FARMS.

RESERVOIR & WATERFALL

HOMES FOR WAIFS.

NEW FOREST

CONCORD

ALLOTMENTS

CENTRAL CITY.

LARGE FARMS.

ALLOTMENTS

RUMSEY

RESERVOIR AND WATERFALL.

GRAND

CANAL

TO THE SEA

ALLOTMENTS

POPULATION 58,000

AREA

ALLOTMENTS

RESERVOIR & WATERFALL

HOME FOR INEBRIATES.

12,000 ACRES

RESERVOIR AND WATERFALL

NEW FORESTS

RESERVOIR & WATERFALL

INTER

INSANE ASYLUM.

INDUSTRIAL HOMES.

AGRICULTURAL COLLEGE

STONE QUARRIES

MUNICIPAL RAILWAY.

RESERVOIR & WATERFALL

RESERVOIR & WATERFALL.

COLLEGE FOR BLIND.

PHILADELPHIA.

RURISVILLE.

RESERVOIR & WATERFALL.

REFERENCE.
ROADS,
RAILROADS,
UNDERGRᵒ Dᵒ
with ROADS over.
CANALS
MUNICIPAL BOUNDARIES

RESERVOIR & WATERFALL

SCALE.
1 Mile   2 Miles.

Conceived as a Utopian response to what he saw as the damaging social and environmental consequences of industrialization, Ebenezer Howard's idea of the Garden City was published in 1898 and captured in this diagram whose symmetry recalls earlier "ideal" city plans.

Character of time or place

OPPOSITE: *These designs by Robert Venturi for the "same" small building exemplified his idea of the "decorated shed"—a cheap building with a styled-up front. By divorcing "style" from structure and function, he wittily challenged central tenets of Modern architecture.*

BELOW LEFT: *Built in the 1920s using wood from two Royal Navy ships, the Liberty of London building reflected Arthur Liberty's desire to create the feeling that while in his store you were walking around your own home—and for the British in the 1920s no style said "home" more clearly than half-timbered Tudor.*

IDEA № 33
STYLE

The concept of style to denote the idea that the art or architecture of a particular period shared a recognizable set of characteristics is recent. It stems from the so-called "father of art history," the German scholar Johann Joachim Winckelmann (1717–68) who proposed an influential biological conception of styles as having a birth, maturity, decline, and eventually disappearance and death.

In Winckelmann's view the mature or "classic" phase offered the clearest and best definition of a style. This idea was, however, rejected by Heinrich Wölfflin (1864–1945) whose widely read *Principles of Art History* (1915) defined period styles by contrasting different uses of the same formal elements—it is said that in presenting his ideas Wölfflin invented the now almost ubiquitous use of paired images in lectures.

The belief that a style has its own "life," and therefore history, was argued by Alois Riegl in his book *Stilfragen*. This opposed both the view associated with the followers of Gottfried Semper, who sought to ground style in specific materials and techniques, and the perennial idea that the origins of art lay in the imitation of nature. By severing stylistic development from such external influences Riegl suggested that styles change out of inner necessity, implying that the absolute aesthetic norms frequently claimed for Classicism had to be dropped, and that **form** could be studied independently of content.

Although the views of style developed during the nineteenth and early twentieth centuries still dominate popular histories of architecture, recent thinking emphasizes that all history is a form of narrative or story-telling. The American philosopher Berel Lang, for example, has written that style is "a version of fiction—a narrative form—tied to the literary trope of synecdoche in which one feature is an ingredient in all the others."

Early attempts to classify past architectural styles reflected a growing interest in previous architecture, and together they had a far-reaching impact on the practice of architecture. By the 1840s in England, for example, architects were drawing on various phases of English medieval, Elizabethan, or Tudor architecture, not to mention several versions of Classicism, having previously revived both Greek and Egyptian forms. This stylistic promiscuity led to growing concern that the century would lack a "style of its own"—a lack made all the more worrying by the growing popularity of the philosophical idea of the **Zeitgeist**.

Although many architects relished the freedom to choose a style freely—some would even offer alternative styles for the elevations of the same plan—others, such as A. W. N. Pugin in England and Eugène Emmanuel Viollet-le-Duc in France—favored a more **organic** view by seeking to ground design in the rational use of materials and construction. Both believed this rationality was epitomized by medieval Gothic and this understanding led Viollet-le-Duc to argue that new materials such as cast and wrought **iron** would inevitably lead to a new style. ■

Following Palladio's Classical example

IDEA № 34

PALLADIANISM

The Venetian Andrea Palladio (1508–80) is the only architect to have given his name to a recognized style. Based on a strict interpretation of the formal principles underpinning Greek and Roman temple architecture, his work's influence spread worldwide thanks to the publication of his *I Quattro Libri dell'Architettura* (The Four Books of Architecture).

Palladio's vision of the ideal villa, seen at its most potent in the Villa Rotonda (above), was to prove hugely influential both on later dwellings such as Chiswick House (1726–29, opposite above), the home of Lord Burlington, and on public buildings, such as the Rotunda that housed the library of the University of Virginia (1822–26, opposite below) in the original buildings planned by Thomas Jefferson.

These combined practical advice on building, systematic rules for design, and, most influentially, measured drawings of both ancient Roman buildings and Palladio's own projects. They also introduced the use of temple fronts on houses and secular buildings, which some saw as a profanation, and the so-called Palladian window. This consists of a central light with a semicircular **arch**, carried on an impost consisting of a small entablature, under which, and enclosing smaller lights on each side, are pilasters. Also known as a Venetian or Serlian window, it had in fact been in use in Rome well before any of these putative "sources," courtesy of the architect Bramante.

Palladio's work exerted an influence throughout Europe in the sixteenth century and found particular favor in England, where the exuberance of Italian Baroque was less eagerly embraced than elsewhere. Adopted early, in 1616, by Inigo Jones for the Queen's House at Greenwich, it flourished a century later. Eighteenth-century Palladianism was promoted by various publications, most influential among them Colen Campbell's *Vitruvius Britannicus* (1715) and the *Quattro Libri* themselves, which were translated into English by Giacomo Leoni and Nicolas Dubois from 1715 to 1720. Campbell's book proved popular among the wealthy patrons for whom he built several country houses, including the influential Stourhead (see p.84), which was also home to one of the most celebrated gardens of its day.

Central to the spread of Palladianism were the aristocratic Richard Boyle, third Earl of Burlington, and his protegé William Kent. Together they pioneered what would become known as the English Landscape Garden, a riposte to the absolutism of the French gardens (and style of government) that Burlington detested. Burlington's own residence, Chiswick House (opposite above), was designed in 1729 as a reinterpretation of Palladio's Villa Rotonda (above), but largely stripped of ornamentation—a feature of English Palladianism characteristic also of Holkham Hall in Norfolk. It was at Holkham that Kent established what was to become another familiar feature—attached wings that assumed almost the same significance as the house itself.

The Palladian style proved equally influential in the U.S. Thomas Jefferson (1743–1826), president and amateur architect, referred to the *Quattro Libri* as his architectural bible. He adopted their principles in designing his family's Monticello estate and the University of Virginia (opposite below), which remains arguably the outstanding architectural ensemble in North America. The great plantation houses of the South were generally Palladian in style, often based on engravings that passed among builders, and not surprisingly—given the climate—the temple front portico proved an imposing and practical centerpiece. With its adoption, in an Irish-inspired variant, for the White House in Washington, D.C. (1792–1800), the importance of Palladianism in defining the image of American democracy was sealed. ■

"Palladianism introduced the use of temple fronts on houses and secular buildings."

The internal thoroughfare

IDEA № 35
CORRIDOR

"The client," Louis Kahn observed, "thinks in terms of corridors, the architect finds reasons for galleries." Surprisingly, given its ubiquity in the planning of modern buildings, it was not until around 1600 that the corridor came into use. Prior to that, rooms had been connected to each other *en suite*, or via a shared hall.

The first example of corridor planning appeared in 1597, at Beaufort House in London designed by John Thorpe, and the corridor became increasingly common after 1630 in the houses of the rich, for whom it offered an effective means of separating members of the household, guests, domestic staff, and servants. Coleshill in Berkshire, built by Sir Roger Pratt in 1630–57, exemplifies the combination of entrance hall, grand open stair, corridors, and backstairs as forms of independent circulation which, combined with a central hall passing through the middle of the building along the length of the plan, permitted access to rooms and separated the servants from the wealthy inhabitants. The major rooms were interconnected to form an enfilade; the corridor ran parallel to them, and the separation of classes it permitted was novel.

The corridor not only segregated classes, it also permitted a growing sense of privacy, turning the (public) room into a (private) closet, thereby anticipating the modern desire for "a room of one's own" and the need to exclude others. In the eighteenth century, however, the family's rooms were still generally interconnected, and it was only with the development of the Victorian ideal of the family that house-planning became the organization of routes and destinations, anticipating the "functional" planning of many building-types in the twentieth century, replete with sterile, artificially lit corridors, such as that opposite.

The most influential architect in this development was Robert Kerr. Like Alberti before him, Kerr disliked the chaos of family life, with its mixing of servants, noise of children, and "prattle of women," but whereas Alberti relied on locks, doors, and the distance between rooms to secure a degree of calm, Kerr favored the compartmentalization of increasingly specialized rooms, differentiated by age, class, and gender, and organized around a complex network of circulation that made them individually private but universally accessible. The "thoroughfare" plan that resulted is seen in its fully developed form in his most ambitious country house, Bearwood in Berkshire, completed in 1864.

Corridor-planning created a network of routes. This prevented the distraction of events occurring within rooms, or between adjacent rooms, that was an inevitable feature of the interconnected-rooms arrangement, while bringing the farthest reaches of a house into effective proximity. The paradox was that by facilitating communication between rooms the corridor reduced contact between people. ∎

TOP: *Largely rebuilt in the mid-eighteenth century by Flitcroft and Holland, Woburn Abbey features a relatively late example of the enfilade of connected rooms that was shortly to be displaced by a separate corridor.*

ABOVE: *Founded in the fifteenth century and comprehensively remodeled in the seventeenth, Tredegar House was reconfigured in the nineteenth century to meet the family's demand for greater privacy using a network of corridors such as that seen here.*

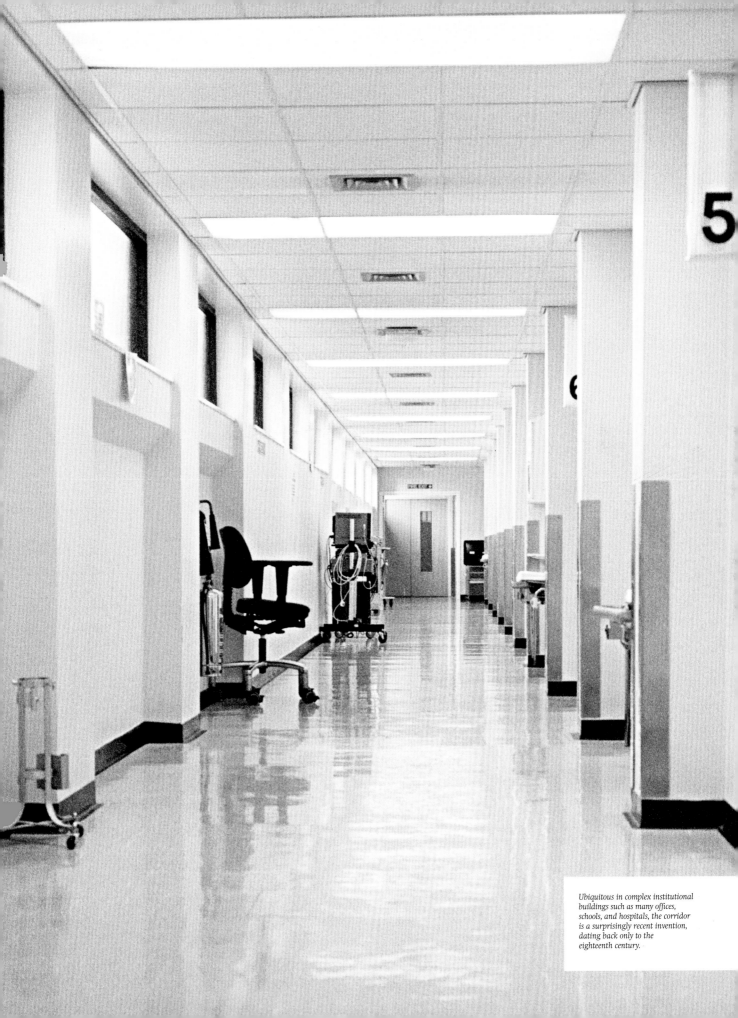

Ubiquitous in complex institutional buildings such as many offices, schools, and hospitals, the corridor is a surprisingly recent invention, dating back only to the eighteenth century.

The sauna at Alvar Aalto's Villa Mairea (1937–40) was inspired by Japanese teahouses and designed to recall memories of traditional Finnish wooden buildings: its "primitive" aura evokes the "return to nature" that is part of the experience of the sauna.

Ancient architectural archetype

IDEA № 36
PRIMITIVE HUT

The idea of the primitive hut stems from Vitruvius's *Ten Books of Architecture*, but owes its place in architectural theory to the *Essay on Architecture* published by the Abbé Laugier in 1753. Advocating the "honest" structural use of the **Classical Orders**, Laugier proposed a cleansing of architecture by returning to its origins.

ABOVE: *Rebuilt every 20 years, the main shrine buildings at Ise in Japan are thought to date back to the sixth century, perpetuating an ancient form modeled on primitive rural buildings.*

BELOW: *The most celebrated "primitive hut" in architectural history appeared in 1755 as a frontispiece to the second edition of the Abbé Laugier's* Essay on Architecture *and purports to show the "natural" origins of the Greek temple.*

As depicted in his engraving (right), he situated these origins in a quasi-natural structure of four tree trunks, neatly growing to a roughly rectangular plan, with logs for lintels and branches creating an elementary pitched roof.

Laugier viewed the primitive hut as the prototype for all great architecture, most obviously the Greek temple, and this led to archaeological efforts to rediscover early examples where the orders were used for construction rather than applied to a wall for decorative effect, as in much Roman and Renaissance architecture. Suitably primitive Greek temples were found at Paestum and the primitive hut was elevated to the status of a type by advocates of Neoclassicism. Equally, Laugier's "back to fundamentals" approach made his ideas congenial to reforming Modernists who sought to strip architecture of stylistic baggage and advocated the "rational" expression of structure.

Beyond the story begun by Vitruvius, the primitive hut has figured in many cultures as a counterpoint to the supposed excesses of civilized life. The Greek Skeptic Diogenes (c.412–323 BC) famously wore ragged clothes and lived in a barrel (actually a large clay pot), while admirers of the seventeenth-century Japanese haiku poet, Basho, built him a rudimentary shelter, drawing on a 3,000-year-old tradition in the Far East of the hut as a site for poetic or philosophical tradition. During the same period in Japan, the Sukiya style modeled on vernacular rural buildings rose to prominence as a counter to the excesses of the wealthy, militaristic shoguns.

In northern and eastern Europe the weekend hut in the country—such as the Russian *dacha*—has long been a valued retreat from the city back to nature. The American writer Henry David Thoreau (1817–62) experimented with a two-year spell living in a determinedly simple house, while the philosopher Martin Heidegger, whose ideas on **phenomenology** have been widely influential in recent architectural theory, worked in a rural hut, following, as Adam Sharr has observed, in a tradition that includes "the Tübingen tower of Friedrich Hölderlin; Johann Wolfgang Goethe's picturesque *Gartenhaus* in Weimar; and Friedrich Nietzsche's mountain convalescent home at Sils Maria in the Swiss Alps." It is not so far in spirit from these exalted examples to the modern fascination with the humble garden shed as a place to write or pursue a hobby.

The most distinguished modern essay in the tradition of the primitive hut is the only house Le Corbusier built for himself, a vacation retreat at Cap Martin (1954–57) consisting of two small buildings made of wood—logs for the dwelling, wooden planks for the studio. He called it La Baraque de Chantier in honor of its model, a workers' shed from a building site, but the exquisite detailing was comparable to the finest Sukiya-style teahouse. ∎

The spirit of the place

IDEA Nº 37
GENIUS LOCI

In ancient Greece and Rome many gods were associated with specific shrines, groves, and springs, while a spirit that had no name was known to the Romans as a genius loci. This referred to the protective spirit itself—not, as later, to the physical atmosphere or environmental quality supposedly embedded in the locality.

The idea of the genius loci entered the English language courtesy of the Romans but its origins predate them: in Predynastic Egypt, for example, the forces of nature were identified with specific gods, and temples were aligned axially with the solar path and other natural features.

The eventual ubiquity of the idea of "spirit" or "sense of place" in architecture and landscape design can be traced to the English poet Alexander Pope. In his "Epistle IV," dedicated to Richard Boyle, Earl of Burlington and leading advocate of English Palladianism, Pope advised would-be exponents of the emerging art of landscape gardening to:

> Consult the genius of the place in all;/
> That tells the waters or to rise, or fall;/Or
> helps th' ambitious hill the heav'ns to scale,/
> Or scoops in circling theatres the vale;/Calls
> in the country, catches opening glades,/
> Joins willing woods, and varies shades from
> shades,/Now breaks, or now directs, th'
> intending lines;/Paints as you plant, and,
> as you work, designs.

Pope's advice was not only followed by landscape gardeners such as Lancelot "Capability" Brown and Humphrey Repton, but also, implicitly, by exponents of **Picturesque** architecture from John Nash to Frank Lloyd Wright, and beyond. It also laid the foundation for a widely agreed principle of landscape architecture that eventually manifested itself as a form of landscape "Functionalism" that maintained a "design" could be largely determined through systematic site analysis. Initiated by Patrick Geddes, this approach came to be associated with Ian McHarg who, in his widely influential book *Design with Nature* (1969), proposed a systematic design method based on combining "natural factors" such as topography, climate, biology, and geology with "human factors" like land uses and settlement patterns.

In architecture, the idea of responding to the genius loci has been widely espoused. The proponents of Italian Neo-Rationalism, such as Aldo Rossi and Giorgio Grassi, grounded their projects in what they saw as a "scientific" reading of a site's history, while in the Italian-speaking region of Switzerland, the Ticino, a movement known as the Tendenza sought to continue the *tendenza* or trends apparent in the land. Mario Botta's house at Riva San Vitale (1971–73, opposite), for example, recalls the towerlike country homes that were once familiar in the region, and its materials reflect the masonry traditions of local farm buildings.

Concern with the genius loci is now largely associated with broader, **Postmodern** thinking on the importance of context, and in particular with ideas indebted to the philosophy of **phenomenology**. This is apparent, for example, in the title of Christian Norberg-Schulz's book, *Genius Loci: Towards a Phenomenology of Architecture*, in which he advocates engagement with the topography of the Earth's surface, the "cosmology" of sky and light, and the symbolic and existential meanings embodied in the cultural landscape as fundamental to human "dwelling." ∎

"Consult the genius of the place in all."

The idea of the "genius loci" continues to inspire architects. The Swiss architect Mario Botta speaks of "building the site": his design for a house at Riva San Vitale (1971–73) is both an observatory from which to enjoy the landscape and a formal response to the mountainous terrain.

Architecture as a stage set

SCENOGRAPHY

Strictly defined, scenography is the practice of making the setting for a theatrical performance. The word itself is of Greek origin, coming from *skini*, meaning stage and *grapho*, meaning to write or describe, and when it came into use in architecture it referred to perspective drawing or scene-painting.

In his designs for London's Regent Street (1811, later entirely rebuilt) John Nash deployed symmetrical, palacelike Classical fronts to create a scenographic composition based on Picturesque principles.

The most celebrated Early Renaissance illustrations of stage sets appeared in Sebastiano Serlio's *De Architettura* published in 1545 and depicted the tragic, comic, and satiric styles described by Vitruvius. The Roman theater also inspired Andrea Palladio's posthumously completed Teatro Olimpico in Vicenza (opposite), in which he reintroduced the *frons scenae* —source of the modern proscenium arch—both as an architectural setting for the dramatic performance and as the frame for illusionistic scenery constructed according to the rules of **perspective** projection.

Architectural effects that began in the theater were extended to the world of real building. In Baldassare Longhena's masterpiece, the Church of

Santa Maria della Salute (1631–87) at the entrance to the Grand Canal in Venice, for example, the familiar elements of Renaissance Classicism are arranged not according to a strictly internal logic, but to present to the strategically situated viewer arrangements that are coherent only when seen in perspective.

Longhena is now widely credited with originating the type of scenographic architecture that became a defining feature of the Late Baroque of the eighteenth century, and in the nineteenth century entire urban ensembles were conceived in this way. In John Nash's design for Regent Street in London (above), for example, the succession of palace fronts was calculated to be seen in acute

perspective as an episodic series of events. Such an approach was related to the tradition of **Picturesque** design that began with eighteenth-century English Landscape Gardens, although the originators of the Picturesque were committed to asymmetry and opposed to the Renaissance values that Nash embraced in many of his buildings.

Recently, the term scenographic has been adopted as an approach by architects critical of orthodox Modern architects' preoccupation with grounding form in functional requirements and constructional logic. Many of Moore, Lyndon, Turnbull, and Whitaker's (MLTW) later projects, such as Kresge College at University of California, Santa Cruz, California (1972–74), were overtly conceived as

Modeled on Roman prototypes, Andrea Palladio's Teatro Olimpico in Vicenza (1579–85) was designed to create the perfect illusion of streets receding into the distance—the stage sets were completed after Palladio's death in 1580 by Vincenzo Scamozzi.

"Architectural effects that began in the theater were extended to the world of real building."

"stages" for communal life, while Robert Venturi's analysis of the Las Vegas strip and conception of the decorated **shed** led him to write an essay entitled "Towards a scenographic architecture for today," in conscious echo of the English title of one of the preeminent Modernist texts, Le Corbusier's *Vers une architecture* ("Towards a New Architecture").

More commonly, "scenographic" has acquired negative connotations by implying the separation of appearance from constructional substance typical of **Postmodern** architecture. Advocating a "critical **regionalism**," for example, Kenneth Frampton berated the "reduction of architecture to a scenography which makes a very gratuitous, or parodied, use of historicist motifs"—a tendency admirably illustrated by Michael Graves' Portland Public Services Building (1980, see p.168), with its representations of giant pilasters and keystones. The influential Finnish architect and critic Juhani Pallasmaa

likewise rejects as scenographic the attempts by planning authorities to promote historical local styles, dubbing the results "sentimental provincialism." ∎

"The Picturesque mediated between
two older aesthetic categories, the
beautiful and the sublime."

A "picture-like" composition

With its freely asymmetrical arrangement and flourish of turrets intended to evoke memories of medieval castles, Downton Castle (completed c.1778 to designs by its owner Richard Payne Knight) was conceived as an avowedly Picturesque composition.

IDEA № 39
PICTURESQUE

The fully developed idea of the Picturesque was introduced by William Gilpin in 1782 in his book *Observations on the River Wye*. To qualify as Picturesque a scene should be rough, intricate, varied, broken, and without obvious straight lines, while exhibiting a picture-like composition.

The paintings of Claude Lorrain and Nicolas Poussin provided models for such scenes and they were often enhanced by a ruined abbey or castle. When these were lacking it became common to construct a folly, often in the form of a ruin.

In his book *The True Principles of Pointed or Christian Architecture*, published in London in 1841, A. W. N. Pugin wrote that "an architect should exhibit his skill by turning the difficulties which occur in raising an elevation from a convenient plan into so many picturesque beauties."

A "convenient" plan usually deviated from the **symmetry** that had governed most architecture. In inviting architects to celebrate this, Pugin was drawing on an aesthetic ideal that grew out of, and reacted to, the English Landscape Garden codified by Lancelot "Capability" Brown (1716–83).

The Picturesque mediated between two older aesthetic categories, the beautiful and the sublime, and its excesses were ridiculed by Jane Austen in *Northanger Abbey*. Describing the aesthetic education of Catherine Morland, she explains that she "was so

hopeful a scholar, that when they gained the top of Beechen Cliff, she voluntarily rejected the whole city of Bath, as unworthy to make part of a landscape."

The rise of the Picturesque sensibility was linked to wider cultural trends—interest in the historic past that led, among other things, to the Gothic Revival, and a fascination with the primitive and exotic, notably China —and the first overtly Picturesque building preceded Gilpin's travel guide. It was begun in 1774 by Richard Payne Knight on the border of Shropshire and Herefordshire and he called it Downton Castle (above). It was planned to be irregular from the outset and represents an important landmark in the development of architecture.

Most thoroughgoing practitioner of the Picturesque in architecture was perhaps John Nash, whose **scenographic** planning of London's Regent's Park created, to quote Sir John Summerson, "dream palaces, full of grandiose, romantic ideas such as an architect might scribble in a holiday sketch book. Seen at a distance, framed in green tracery, perhaps in the kind

light of autumn, they suggest architectural glories which make Greenwich tame and Hampton Court provincial"—qualities not so apparent, as Summerson went on to point out, in the endless repetition of houses in the streets behind the public fronts.

Although its excesses could border on the absurd, the legacy of the Picturesque was substantial. It contributed to the rise of the Garden City movement, with its belief in the importance of ready access to countryside; promoted the principle of the "convenient" or irregular plan which, via the Arts and Crafts movement, contributed to the development of the Modern, functional plan; and it encouraged the idea that a building should "fit" by being organically related to the site. ∎

"The true principles of pointed architecture"

IDEA № 40
GOTHIC REVIVAL

Gothic Revival design can be seen at its most romantic at Cardiff Castle in Wales and, a few miles to the north, Castell Coch (1871–91), seen below. Both were commissioned by the Marquis of Bute and designed by William Burges.

Art-historically, Gothic refers to a style that originated around Paris in the court circles of France in the late twelfth century, and spread across Europe, lasting well into the sixteenth century. It was characterized by prodigious structural innovation based on the pointed arch, ribbed vault, and flying buttress. Gothic reemerged in the late eighteenth century, leading to the Gothic Revival in the nineteenth.

Gothic was originally known as the French style, and the word was used as an insult in the 1530s by the Italian Renaissance critic Giorgio Vasari. Although some historians argue that Gothic never died out, being preserved in the practice of stonemasons, it is generally regarded as having died out during the seventeenth century and much of the eighteenth before being revived, when it found particular favor among advocates of the **Picturesque**. The pioneer in this respect was the writer Horace Walpole (1717–97) who acquired his "little play-thing house," Strawberry Hill (opposite), in Twickenham near London, in 1748 and transformed it into a Gothic fantasy. His designers John Chute (1701–76), and Richard Bentley (1708–82) created an eclectic mix of turrets and battlements derived from castles and the ecclesiastical Gothic style.

Walpole's fantasy house was influential in promoting interest in Gothic, but the fully fledged Gothic Revival of the nineteenth century initially had an altogether more serious tone. Ideologically, it was linked to the reformist Oxford Movement that promoted the "high church" Anglo-Catholic liturgy, while architecturally it came to stand for a commitment to the "honest" expression of structure and use of materials. In his 1841 book *The True Principles of Pointed or Christian Architecture*, for example, A. W. N. Pugin wrote that "the two great rules for design are these: first, that there should be no features about a building which are not necessary for convenience, construction or propriety; second, that all ornament should consist of the essential construction of the building." He went on to explain that "the architects of the Middle Ages were the first who turned the natural properties of the various materials to their full account, and made their mechanism a vehicle for their art."

Although he denied any debt to Pugin, these ideas were echoed in John Ruskin's extensive writings, while in France the greatest theorist of the age, Eugène Emmanuel Viollet-le-Duc, argued that employing materials "according to their qualities and properties" was essential to being "true to the constructive processes" which are the basis of architecture—principles he sought to demonstrate in structures that exploited the properties of stone and **iron** in combination. He was less persuasive as a designer than writer, however, and it is through his ten-volume *Dictionary of Architecture*—in effect, a history of French Gothic—and the two-volume edition of his lectures, that Viollet-le-Duc exerted major influence. Frank Lloyd Wright presented the lectures to his son John Lloyd with the commendation, "in these volumes you will find all the architectural schooling you will ever need" and Viollet-le-Duc has justifiably been called "the first theorist of modern architecture." His vision of Gothic "truth" contributed substantially to the belief that a new architecture would grow from the rigorous expression of industrial materials, a belief expressed—albeit variously—in both art nouveau and the early Modern Movement. ∎

After purchasing Strawberry Hill in 1748, Horace Walpole set about a comprehensive transformation. Externally he looked to medieval castles as models, while internally—as seen in this fan vault—he favored English Gothic church architecture. The house is now widely seen as anticipating the Gothic Revival that flourished in the nineteenth century.

"The Beaux-Arts system of education proved widely influential, particularly in the U.S."

Designed by Charles Garnier, the Paris Opéra was one of the grandest buildings realized in the academic Beaux-Arts style that dominated French architecture and teaching in the mid-nineteenth century.

Academic style of rich ornament and strict method

IDEA № 41
BEAUX-ARTS

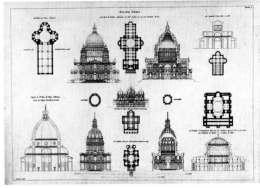

Beaux-Arts refers to both an ornamented style of nineteenth-century architecture and to the educational institution in which it developed, founded as the Académie des Beaux-arts in Paris in 1648.

In 1671 the Académie Royale d'Architecture was established by France's finance minister Jean-Baptiste Colbert and the architect François Blondel; in 1863 Napoléon III granted it independence from the government, and it merged with other academies to become the Ecole des Beaux-arts.

The Ecole's focus was on Classical arts and architecture, and the curriculum was divided between painting and sculpture, and architecture. The school also marked a separation between architecture and the practical business of building—the latter being addressed through the Ecole Nationale des Ponts et Chaussées and the Ecole Polytechnique, which remains one of the world's great engineering schools.

The Beaux-Arts system of education proved widely influential, particularly in the U.S., where many universities—led by the Massachusetts Institute of Technology (MIT) in 1892—adopted its methods and employed its graduates. Several leading American architects studied in Paris—among them Richard Morris Hunt, Charles Follen McKim (of McKim, Mead, and White), and Henry Hobson Richardson—and the acclaimed "White City" at the 1893 World's Columbian Exposition was considered a triumph of the Beaux-Arts style. Many universities, including Columbia in New York, MIT, and Berkeley in California, were designed by leading exponents of the style, as were several major railroad stations including notably New York's Grand Central.

Just as influential as the richly ornamented, academic style of Classicism that it promoted were the Ecole's teaching methods. Students were divided into "ateliers" run by practicing architects—which finds an echo in the modern "unit system"—and at the core of the method was the *esquisse*, or preliminary design sketch. Produced in a short time period (usually under ten hours), without the aid of books or advice and working *en loge* (in a small, private cubicle), the key to the *esquisse* was the choice of parti— akin to today's "organizing idea" or "diagram."

The repertoire of possible partis was limited, and in developing their *esquisses* students would deploy a range of formalized techniques, originally based on the idea of (functional) *distributions*, modeled on Vitruvius's ideas, but later developed into the more all-embracing concept of **composition**. A notable feature of Beaux-Arts projects was *poché*, voids "pocketed" within the solid structure of the building, which were used to model space but not necessarily required for structural stability. This use of *poché* may well have contributed to Louis Kahn's idea of **servant and served space**; he had experienced the Beaux-Arts system at the University of Pennsylvania.

The students' final projects were presented using large, highly elaborate drawings rendered in watercolor to show the modeling of **space** and **form** by light. They were carried, generally at the last minute, *en charrette* (in a wheeled trolley that has given its name to a rapid sketch design or short competition) for consideration by a jury. If the jury determined that the final design departed from the intent of the original *esquisse* the project would be deemed *hors de concours* (out of the competition) and not allowed to contribute to the credits needed for graduation. ■

TOP: *The exterior of Garnier's Paris Opéra.*

ABOVE: *Although he taught at a different institution, the systematic pedagogical and compositional methods of Jean-Nicolas-Louis Durand eventually did much to spread the Ecole des Beaux-arts' academic system. Here we see a spread from one of his books published in 1830 comparing different church designs.*

Founding material of the Industrial Revolution

SUPPLEMENT (GRATIS) TO THE ILLUSTRATED LONDON NEWS, NOVEMBER 16, 1850.

The construction of the Crystal Palace in six months in 1851 was a tour de force *of industrial construction using "off-site" components of cast and wrought iron and glass; in size and speed it has not been equaled.*

IDEA № 42

IRON

The smelting of iron to make weapons is thought to have begun in the twelfth century BC, but its production in sufficient quantities to be of widespread use in building construction had to await the Industrial Revolution.

The large-scale production of iron began in England in the early eighteenth century, and began to find its way into building in the 1770s. The puddling process for making wrought iron was invented in 1784, and a skilled worker could make up to a ton a day. The rolling techniques that were later applied to steel soon followed, and were used initially for railroad tracks, later for structural members.

Iron was ideal for industrial structures such as cotton mills and warehouses, where it was combined with brick exterior walls to create multistory constructions that were fire-resistant. By the mid-nineteenth century iron could be seen, as the Scottish writer and reformer Samuel Smiles (1812–1904) wrote in 1863, as "not only the soul of every other manufacture, but the mainspring, perhaps, of civilized society." In France the architect and theorist Eugène Emmanuel Viollet-le-Duc argued that the key to progress lay in coming to terms with industrial materials. For such advocates of architecture as the **art of building** rather than an abstract art of **form** or **space**, iron was seen as the harbinger of the long-awaited expression of the **Zeitgeist**. Its potential was apparent in the market halls, greenhouses, and railroad stations designed by engineers; while not considered "architecture" by many, they were undeniably impressive.

The first full exposure of an iron structure in a public building came in Paris in 1850, in Henri Labrouste's Bibliothèque Ste. Geneviève (opposite): its iron barrel-vault was a conventional form and highly ornamented, but it was still a provocative challenge to expectations. For many, however, the assimilation of iron into architecture posed a serious aesthetic problem. Inspired by the widely espoused theory of **empathy**, the German architect Ludwig Bohnstedt doubted if the use of iron would lead to a new style. "Our traditional laws of style," he wrote, "are rooted precisely in our experiences with a solid material—with stone—and have been made to harmonize with it; those laws determine the fulfillment of all demands, which up to now *only stone* has been able to satisfy."

Attempting to counter such arguments, one of iron's early advocates in Germany, Edvard Metzger, wrote that while he could understand that "iron construction is an abomination to the sculpturally minded architect," nevertheless the "slim and graceful contours, striving upward, strong or delicate according to circumstance" which iron permitted promised a new kind of beauty. Even Karl Bötticher, whose three-volume book *Die Tektonik der Hellenen* (1843–52) was a major exposition of the virtues of Greek **tectonics**, declared iron the material of the future, suggesting that the Greek and Gothic styles had nearly "run their course" and that the foundations of a "third style" were being laid. Despite such impressive achievements as London's Crystal Palace (above) and Paris' Eiffel Tower, the realization of that style would depend on a material that overcame iron's weakness in tension: **steel**. ∎

The reading room of Henri Labrouste's Bibliothèque of Ste. Geneviève in Paris, completed in 1850, combined traditional-looking vaults with the first use of exposed iron construction in a public building.

The Hong Kong and Shanghai Bank
(1979–86), designed by Foster and
Partners, exploits the tensile strength
of steel by suspending the floor slabs
from a series of external trusses.

The material of the modern frame

STEEL

The strength of steel made possible the development of the early high-rise buildings of Chicago; the first all-steel frame appeared in 1891 in the Ludington Building designed by William Le Baron Jenney. In contrast to Europe, where reinforced concrete is still widely used, the frames of tall buildings in the U.S. are built almost exclusively of steel.

In 1855 the Englishman Sir Henry Bessemer patented the simple but revolutionary idea of purifying liquid pig iron by blowing air through it. Steel, hitherto made only in tiny quantities for such specialized uses as sword and knife blades, could now be produced industrially. Used in compression, steel still did not at this point make economic sense in lightly loaded, low-rise buildings, but in the economy of scale of the skyscraper it did.

Rolled, drawn, and hollow steel sections are now used at a vast variety of sizes, from primary structure, to cladding and window systems, to all manner of fixings, while steel rods and meshes are the basis of **reinforced concrete** construction. The properties of steel can also be readily modified. Repeatedly rolling sheets or sections, or drawing wires, greatly increases their strength; increasing the amount of carbon doubles or trebles the tensile strength, but with a corresponding increase in brittleness; adding nickel and chromium produces stainless steel.

Most steels do, however, have two major disadvantages: lack of fire-resistance and vulnerability to rust. The latter necessitates the use of galvanizing or coating (with paint, plastics, or other materials), while the former is addressed by encasing steel in masonry, concrete, or lightweight linings, or by using thick intumescent coatings that can be applied like paint. Both encasing and coating were considered problematic by architects committed to "truth to materials." Mies van der Rohe controversially introduced "ornamental" steel I-sections on the outside of his Lake Shore Drive Apartments, built in Chicago between 1948 and 1951, to represent the columns buried in concrete. And for many years architects used only black or gray paint, eschewing color because, it was conjectured by the Dutch architect Aldo van Eyck, this might undermine the "seriousness" of the steelwork's structural role.

A surprising alternative to conventional ways of dealing with rust is to add small amounts of copper, whose own oxidation when exposed to the atmosphere forms a protective layer. Trademarked in the early 1950s by the U.S. Steel Corporation as COR-TEN, corten (or "weathering steel") soon found favor among architects—its first large-scale use was by Eero Saarinen in 1964, on the headquarters for John Deere and Company.

Although steel is immensely strong in compression, its strength-to-weight ratio is most fully exploited by using it in tension. An exoskeleton of slender columns, struts, and tension cables is a familiar feature of many of the glamorous High-tech **sheds** built by architects such as Norman Foster,

No building better epitomizes the potential of steel construction than New York's Empire State Building (1930–31): at 102 stories it was for 40 years the world's tallest building and, remarkably, took only 14 months to build.

Richard Rogers, and their followers, while the structure of Foster's Hong Kong and Shanghai Bank (1979–86, opposite) was based on suspending floors from giant trusses using slender hangers rather than supporting them from below with heavier columns.

IDEA № 44

GLASS

A seemingly magical product of heating silica, lime, and an alkali such as soda or potash, glass has been made since the Bronze Age, but for most of its history it remained a luxury material. It was not until the second half of the twentieth century that it was fully exploited as a building material.

The medieval vision of heaven as a city of colored light found exquisite expression in the Gothic interior of the Sainte Chapelle in Paris. Completed in 1246, it was substantially restored in the nineteenth century by Viollet-le-Duc.

The first extensive use of glass in buildings was by the Romans. The cast and blown techniques they developed were widely disseminated, while in Syria during the first three centuries AD the "crown" process, based on spinning a glass disk, was refined. It was only during the Middle Ages, in the valleys of the Seine and Rhine—encouraged by the more northerly climate, and the development of the skeletal Gothic style—that a substantial window-glass industry developed.

Combined with cast and wrought iron and later steel, the industrial production of glass made possible the development of glasshouses, market halls, arcades, and other glass structures—of course, nowhere more spectacularly than in Joseph Paxton's Crystal Palace of 1851 (opposite bottom). In 1914 the Belgian Emile Fourcault developed a vertical-drawing process that enabled the production of larger sheets of glass, which were quickly embraced by Modern architects, but the major revolution in glass-making did not come until 1952 in England when Alastair Pilkington, an employee of the eponymous Lancashire-based firm (and not a relative of its owners), had the revolutionary idea of replacing the rigid bed on which glass was cast with a molten metal; after many experiments, tin proved most suitable.

By 1959 the new "float glass" process was commercially viable and quickly all but replaced earlier glass-making methods. The first generation of plants could not respond to specialized requirements, such as a particular color, because float glass production operates as a continuous process, with an endless ribbon of material flowing off the line at approximately 50ft (15m) per minute day and night, year after year, until maintenance is required.

The **transparency** made possible by large sheets of glass made it the quintessential material of twentieth-century architecture, a means of revealing—in theory, if not always in practice—the "truth" of the underlying structure and space. The undulating profile of Mies van der Rohe's seminal 1923 Project for a Glass Tower was designed to exploit the other striking visual property of glass—its reflectivity—but it was not until Norman Foster's Willis Faber Dumas Building (1970–75, opposite top) that Mies's idea of hanging a "curtain wall" from the top of a building was realized. ∎

"A seemingly magical product of heating silica, lime, and an alkali."

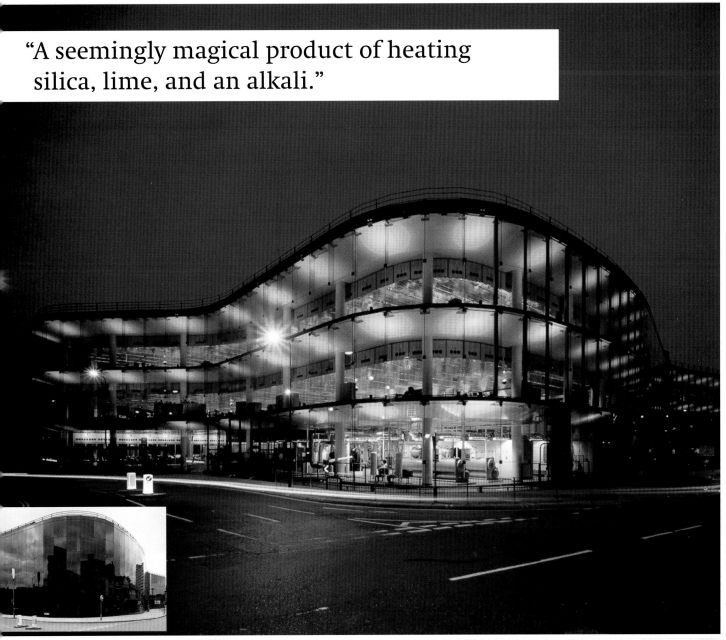

ABOVE: *The Modernist dream of an all-glass curtain wall was finally fulfilled in 1975 with the completion of the Willis Faber Dumas Building in Ipswich, England, by Norman Foster.*

RIGHT: *Built in Hyde Park, London for the Great Exhibition of 1851 and later moved to a site in Sydenham, south London, the Crystal Palace was a dazzling demonstration of the potential of industrialized glass and iron production.*

Light from above

IDEA № 45

ROOF LIGHTING

Due largely to the invention of the Velux "roof window," domestic roofscapes are now frequently spattered with roof lights, while large top-lit **atria** are found in countless offices and other buildings.

Surprisingly, despite its familiarity—and with the glorious exception of the Pantheon (see p.31), whose unglazed oculus is its sole source of light—roof lighting is a relatively recent architectural innovation.

Its potential did not really begin to be exploited until the mid-eighteenth century when developments in glass manufacture made available relatively cheap sheets of adequate size—a practical necessity, as neither wooden frames nor lead cames could be relied upon not to leak. The earliest form of roof light was a sheet of glass inserted into a tiled roof in place of a tile—an idea which was largely confined to utilitarian buildings, but artfully revived by Sverre Fehn in the Bispegaard Museum in Hamar, Norway (1968–88), which occupies a substantially rebuilt barn.

Opening, wood-framed, and lead-clad roof lights can still be found on some eighteenth-century domestic buildings but did not become common in ordinary houses until the late nineteenth century, partly because excise duties imposed on glass by weight favored small, thin panes of glass. The removal of excise duties in the U.K. in 1845 coincided with various improvements in the manufacture of glass. The most noticeable and widespread impact was the removal of glazing bars in windows, but it also encouraged the spread of roof lights.

Mass-produced cast-iron roof lights became widely available and large-scale overhead "patent glazing" was used in buildings from market halls and railroad stations to museums. Deep-plan buildings such as the Leeds Corn Exchange by Cuthbert Brodrich

(1861–64) and the Oxford Museum of Natural History by Deane and Woodward (1855–60) would have been impossible without roof lighting, while at the domestic scale roof lights were most commonly deployed over staircases, often with secondary glazing to reduce cold downdrafts.

Although historically the majority of roof lights were employed for utilitarian reasons, the quality of light they could give was recognized by eighteenth-century architects such as Robert Adam, who used lanterns over staircases and halls to impressive effect. They were also much favored by Sir John Soane. His own house–museum in in London (1792–1827) is a treasure trove of inventive lighting, and his Dulwich Picture Gallery (1811–17, opposite) established the modern type of the top-lit museum and art gallery. Innovative examples include Alvar Aalto's North Jutland Museum of Modern Art (left), where light is reflected off curved structural beams to diffuse evenly over the walls, and Louis Kahn's Kimbell Museum, in which light is admitted via a slot between two curved beams, bounced back up against their undersides, and finally reflected down into the museum. ∎

Designed in 1958, Alvar Aalto's North Jutland Museum of Modern Art pioneered the use of complex rooflighting sections. Designed to create shadowless light, they were refined and widely used in later galleries worldwide.

"The top-lit interior is isolated from
the city outside."

Designed by the engineer William
Le Baron Jenney and built in 1885,
the Home Insurance Building in
Chicago was the first to be supported
by a metal structural frame—a
combination of steel and cast and
wrought iron: it is widely regarded
as the world's first skyscraper.

The building's skeleton

The ever taller buildings that now dominate the skylines of major cities worldwide—such as Shanghai, seen here—are made possible by two nineteenth-century innovations: the elevator and the steel or reinforced concrete structural frame.

IDEA Nº 46
STRUCTURAL FRAME

Structural frames have been widely used throughout history where wood was readily available as a building material. Cast-iron framed buildings came with the Industrial Revolution, when textile factories required large-span, open spaces for machinery. In the nineteenth century the advent of steel frames led to the world's first skyscrapers in the U.S.

In Europe, despite the widespread use of wooden box frame (half-timbered) construction, masonry remained dominant well into the twentieth century, while the earliest buildings to abandon load-bearing walls in favor of a framework of stone columns and ribs—the Gothic cathedrals—were eclipsed by the revival of Classical architecture. With the development of low-cost and structurally reliable cast iron in the second half of the eighteenth century the means to deliver iron-framed, open-plan factories became available. Wrought iron replaced cast iron in the mid-nineteenth century, enabling the construction of Joseph Paxton's spectacular Crystal Palace (see p.90) for London's Great Exhibition of 1851.

With the invention of industrial processes to turn **iron** into **steel**, the preeminent material of modern framed structures was made available and affordable. The first steel section handbook was issued by Dorman (later Dorman Long) in 1887, and Sir William Arrol, who completed the steel-framed rail bridge over the River Forth, north of Edinburgh, Scotland, in 1890, had built more than 140 steel-framed workshops by 1907. London's Ritz Hotel (1904–05) was the city's first fully steel-framed building, but by then tall, steel-framed structures were rising apace in Chicago, where Burnham and Root's Montauk Building (1882–83) was given the name "skyscraper" by the author Erik Larson.

Industrial production of nails and machining of lumber enabled the development of lightweight wooden frames. In the 1830s Chicago builders developed the so-called balloon frame that enabled low-skilled laborers to rapidly assemble a house. Made from 4 by 2in (100 by 50mm) lumber at up to 2ft (600mm) centers and sheathed in plywood, it became ubiquitous in the U.S. by the mid-nineteenth century and was one of the means by which "the West was won." In the U.S. wood-framing remains the dominant form of house construction and, given wood is a **sustainable** material, considerable research is now going into multistory wood-framed buildings.

Architecturally, the structural frame's primary impact was twofold: by exploiting the strength of steel, either as structural sections or in **reinforced concrete**, it enabled the construction of buildings of unprecedented height; and by relieving walls of their load-bearing function it permitted the development of both the **free plan** and lightweight **cladding** systems—the combination that Mies van der Rohe called "skin and bones" architecture. Giving visual expression to the "bones" of the structural frame proved problematic in multistory buildings due to the demands of fire-proofing and the refusal of **glass** to appear transparent during daylight. One solution—seen in Eero Saarinen's John Deere and Company head-quarters—was to recess the skin well behind the outer ring of columns and beams, but this in turn has recently been made problematic by the demand for better environmental performance, precluding the thermal bridges created by continuity of structure. ■

Ancient luxury of the "sitting culture"

ABOVE: *Wrapped around an iron column, this hot-water Victorian radiator in the National Museum of Scotland is an early example of the use of central heating in public buildings.*

IDEA № 47
CENTRAL HEATING

Central heating is almost as old as architecture itself. Its origins probably lie in an ancient Greek system of blowing hot air from furnaces through vents laid into floors, first seen in 350 BC in the Great Temple of Ephesus, but its most celebrated early form was the Roman *hypocaust*.

Consisting of underfloor ducts through which hot air was drawn from flues in the walls, it was initially the preserve of the wealthy but became common in public buildings throughout the Roman Empire. Cistercian monks revived the use of central heating using channeled water and wood furnaces in monasteries such as that of Our Lady of the Wheel (1202) near Aragon, Spain.

The first use of underfloor pipes came in twelfth-century Syria and was later applied in bathhouses across the medieval Islamic world. In the Far East, the Korean Ondol system of underfloor heating is thought to have been enjoyed since the start of the Koguryo period in 37 BC. It originally used hot gases but this gave way to hot-water systems, which are still in use in Korea and are credited with customs such as the removal of shoes and the "sitting culture." Frank Lloyd Wright experienced an Ondol-heated home in Japan in the early twentieth century and decided it was the perfect form of heating: pipes embedded in floor slabs became standard in the Usonian Houses (opposite bottom) he built widely from the mid-1930s.

In Europe central heating was surprisingly rare during the eighteenth and nineteenth centuries. It was largely confined to the aristocracy—a water-based system was installed in the Summer Palace in St. Petersburg (1710–14), for example—or to specialized uses such as the steam-based system installed in the 1830s in the home of the Governor of the Bank of England, where it was used to grow grapes. Later it was widely deployed in warehouses and factories.

By the end of the nineteenth century cheap cast-iron radiators and developments in boiler technology lay the foundations for the central heating systems familiar today. The principle was extended to so-called district heating systems, which generally used waste heat from electricity generation plants to heat thousands of homes. Although known in the West—for example in Pimlico, London—district heating found particular favor in the former Soviet bloc, where centralization was more acceptable.

Central heating systems freed architects from the planning constraints that had been imposed by chimneys, and so facilitated innovations like the **free plan**, but fireplaces continued to be popular as a focus in some living rooms. And as fireplaces disappeared or fell into disuse, the fogs and smogs that were a familiar feature of industrial cities also began to vanish.

Socially, the impact of central heating was revolutionary. Whereas communal family life in lower middle-class and working-class households had centered around one or perhaps two living rooms with their fireplaces, with the advent of central heating bedrooms became usable spaces for children and teenagers. As a consequence, family life became more dispersed and differentiated—a trend accelerated by the advent of widely affordable consumer electronics. ■

"Socially, the impact of central heating was revolutionary."

ABOVE: *The Roman system of a raised floor above a heated hypocaust, seen here at the ruins of the third-century AD Thermae (public baths) at Sbeitla in Tunisia, is one of the earliest forms of central heating.*

LEFT: *Impressed by a Korean system of underfloor heating encountered on a visit to Japan in the early twentieth century, Frank Lloyd Wright made a hot-water-pipe system laid over the floor slab a standard feature of his Usonian Houses.*

LEFT: *So-called "Moonlight Towers" were popular in American and European cities in the late nineteenth century, but were rapidly replaced by street lighting. This archival picture shows a 164ft- (50m-) high example in Austin, Texas, where they are still in use.*

ABOVE: *As early as the 1920s, New York's Times Square was filled with the illuminated advertising that continues to enchant tourists.*

The center of Miami, Florida, epitomizes the image of the contemporary "electric city."

Emblem of the modern age

IDEA Nº 48

ELECTRIC LIGHTING

The search for electric light began in the early nineteenth century but it was not until 1879 that a commercially viable incandescent lightbulb was produced by Thomas Edison in the U.S. Despite its relatively recent invention, electric lighting has become an essential part of how we experience architecture and the urban environment.

The introduction of electric lighting into buildings depended on distribution systems, and the impact of street lighting on cities, courtesy of the arc lamp developed by the Russian Pavel Yablochkov in 1875, was initially greater. In London arc lamps were used to light Holborn Viaduct and the Thames Embankment, while in the U.S. 130,000 were in operation by 1890, at first in Moonlight towers (opposite) used to illuminate large areas from a single point, street lamps being too expensive until the advent of cheaper incandescent fittings.

Light was widely seen as a means of curing illness and preventing physical and social ills—notably crime—and the possibility of lighting entire cities was considered a form of public "sanitation" akin to sewers. For the 1889 Centennial Exhibition in Paris a prominent French architect, Jules Bourdais, proposed a 1,181ft- (360m-) high Tour Soleil (Sun Tower) topped with arc lights intended to illuminate the entire city via satellite reflectors.

Electric light quickly became a preeminent emblem of **Modernity**. It allowed the development of the cinema, and in department stores such as the Magasin du Printemps in Paris, which opened in 1883, was used to promote consumption. Illuminated advertising soon became inseparable from the image of the modern metropolis: as early as 1928, in New York's Times Square, the German architect Ernst May was "dazzled by a profusion of scintillating lights."

Although modern lifestyles and buildings are inconceivable without electric lighting, its impact was far from benign. Fluorescent lamps, which appeared early in the twentieth century, facilitated the development of deep plans that could be inhabited independently of daylight. In the era of cheap energy and stand-alone buildings, this led to almost windowless elevations predicated on the belief that windows were not only distracting to the workers—or, in the case of schools, children—but also, if openable, would interfere with the efficient operation of mechanical ventilation or **air-conditioning** systems.

For many architects, designing for natural light and responding to the movement of the sun became an irrelevance. Elevations ignored orientation, and supposedly "ideal" levels of lighting for given tasks led to uniformly lit spaces that diminished the occupants' sense of orientation and awareness of space. By night, lit from within, such buildings presented an exciting, quintessentially Modern spectacle, but by day they offered few clues as to what might be going on inside, making them and the cities they came to dominate appear almost abandoned.

Eventually, with increasingly costly energy and growing concern about human impacts on the global environment, such high-energy buildings were found to be both uneconomic and unhealthy for their occupants. The spread of the naturally lit **atrium** office building in the 1980s was one response, and architects now generally seek to combine natural and electric light using new, energy-efficient sources such as compact fluorescent lamps (CFLs) and light-emitting diodes (LEDs). ■

A hundred floors into the air

IDEA № 49
THE ELEVATOR

Architectural histories emphasize the **structural frames** that made possible the tall buildings that have transformed cities worldwide. Equally important, however, was the passenger elevator, without which frequent circulation beyond a few stories becomes impracticable.

Completed in 2009 and topping out at more than 1,969ft (600m), the Burj Khaliifa in Dubai, designed by the American architects SOM, is the world's tallest structure. It is served by 57 elevators traveling at speeds of up to 33ft/sec (10m/sec).

The idea of the elevator is ancient: it was mentioned by the Roman architect Vitruvius and a working version was reportedly built by Archimedes around 236 BC. Proto-elevators were installed in palace buildings in England and France in the seventeenth century but the key breakthrough came in 1852 when Elisha Graves Otis invented a reliable safety mechanism.

The first Otis passenger elevator was installed in a New York department store in 1857, and seven years later the Grosvenor became the first London hotel to offer an elevator. Its impact was social as well as practical: the formerly low-grade upper floors of hotels became desirable for their views, leading to the rooftop penthouse suite.

With the development of the first electric elevator by Werner von Siemens in 1880, the key features of the modern elevator were in place. An electric motor driving steel ropes over a drive sheave attached to a gearbox can now move an elevator car at up to 500ft (150m) per minute, while gearless traction elevators are capable of reaching speeds of up to 1,969ft (600m) per minute.

Early elevators were controlled by attendants or manually by their users, but gradually systems were developed to send the elevator efficiently to waiting passengers. As buildings grew in height these became vital. Computer dispatching systems are now capable of "learning" peak-flow patterns and adapting to changing traffic requirements. Architecturally more interesting was the idea of combining express elevators, stopping only at certain floors, with local elevators serving each floor in a given segment of the building. Such a "sky lobby" arrangement was first introduced in SOM's 100-story John Hancock Center in Chicago—located on the 44th floor, the sky lobby serves the residential floors above and provides health, leisure, and educational facilities. Later, in the Hong Kong and Shanghai Bank Building in Hong Kong (see p.92), Norman Foster introduced the idea of double-height "vertical villages" reached by elevators and then served by escalators.

A different attempt to overcome the anonymity of traveling in elevators was to remove the passenger car from its shaft and encapsulate it in glass. This was first proposed by the Vesnin Brothers in their 1924 project for the Pravda Tower, but the first modern glass elevator was installed at the El Cortez Hotel in San Diego, California, as a way of avoiding the disruption of building an internal shaft. Wall-climbing glass elevators would later be widely used, notably at the Lloyds Building in London by Richard Rogers (see p.167). John Portman's Hyatt Regency in Atlanta led the way in 1967, with glass "capsules" ascending to its revolving rooftop restaurant. ∎

"Without elevators, buildings beyond a few stories would be impractical."

ABOVE: *The 1930s offered no more compelling illustration of the intensity of development made possible by the elevator than the New York skyline; the 102-story Empire State Building, seen in the distance, remained the world's tallest until the 1970s.*

FAR LEFT: *Elisha Otis at the Crystal Palace Exposition in New York in 1854, demonstrating the safety mechanism he later patented. It became the key to the elevator's widespread adoption as a means of passenger transportation.*

LEFT: *The Petronas Twin Towers in Kuala Lumpur, which held the title of the world's tallest building from 1998 to 2004, are served by a complex array of Otis elevators, many in "double-decker" format that simultaneously call at adjacent odd and even floors.*

"The best structural material yet devised by mankind."

This wonderfully elegant open-sided aircraft hangar, designed and built by the engineer Pier Luigi Nervi in Orvieto, Italy, in 1935 used a thin concrete shell, strengthened by slender ribs, to span 147ft (44.8m).

"Melted stone of any shape"

IDEA № 50
REINFORCED CONCRETE

ABOVE: *The earliest known concrete was developed by the Romans and used to build many of their greatest vaulted structures—of which this fallen coffered section in the Forum Romanum is a ruined fragment.*

BELOW: *Building inspectors were convinced that the mushroom columns of Frank Lloyd Wright's Johnson Wax Building were too slender. Never one to doubt his ability, Wright sat under a test column while it was piled with sandbags to well beyond the designed load.*

Although it did not have a single inventor, the basis of modern reinforced concrete using steel bars was established in the 1890s by François Hennebique. It was made possible by the fact that the two materials have identical coefficients of thermal expansion, and its use spread rapidly—by 1910 some 40,000 structures are estimated to have been built with it.

The first form of concrete was invented by the Romans and made by mixing quicklime, pozzolanic ash, and pumice aggregate. Called *opus caementicium* it was much weaker in tension than modern concretes and had to be laid by hand rather than poured. It was used in many of the major Roman buildings, including the public baths, the Colosseum (see p.25), and the Pantheon (see p.31). Concrete disappeared with the collapse of the Roman Empire and its modern use depended on the invention of Portland cement, patented in 1824, and the addition of reinforcing.

Reinforced concrete's superiority over steel where there was a fire was vividly demonstrated in 1902 when a fire at the plant of Pacific Coast Borax in Bayonne, New Jersey, left the steel in molten puddles but the reinforced concrete floors still intact. The historian Reyner Banham has suggested this was the catalyst for its widespread take-up, and the grain silos, warehouses, and factories for which it found ready use became icons of modernity in Europe, courtesy of an influential set of photographs published by both Walter Gropius and Le Corbusier, the latter hailing them as examples of "the Engineer's Aesthetic" in his book *Vers une architecture.*

The first use of an exposed concrete frame in a domestic building came in Paris in 1903 with an apartment building in Rue Franklin by Auguste and Gustave Perret. Le Corbusier worked for Auguste Perret five years later and initially looked to reinforced concrete as a means of creating sleek new visions of the Machine Age. When this proved problematic, he later advocated the use of rough **béton brut** as a more "natural" expression of the material.

It fell mainly to a succession of great engineers—Robert Maillart, Eugène Freyssinet, Pier Luigi Nervi, Eduardo Torroja, and Felix Candela, among others—to exploit the clarity of structural expression the material made possible. To Nervi, concrete was "the best structural material yet devised by mankind. Almost by magic, we have been able to create 'melted' stones of any desired shape." The shapes he desired were those that expressed the forces at work, but to architects determined to work "**in the nature of materials,**" concrete seemed more problematic. In Britain it was initially considered a "pagan" material, lacking a "nature" of its own and unsuitable for the popular neo-Gothic style. Even Frank Lloyd Wright, whose Unity Temple in Oak Park, Chicago, was among the first major achievements in the material, initially declared that concrete had "neither song nor story" and amounted to "an artificial stone at best, or a petrified sand heap at worst." He eventually decided that its true

"nature" lay in the fluidity and continuity it allowed. His Fallingwater House (see p.61) and Johnson Wax Building (above) were two of the great expressive achievements in the material. ∎

"The 'new' materials of iron, steel, and glass were promoted as models for architecture."

Supremely elegant structures such as Gustave Eiffel's Garabit Viaduct (1884) were seen as exemplars by progressive architects eager to promote their vision of architecture as "the art of building."

The aesthetics of construction

ART OF BUILDING

By the late nineteenth century the "mere buildings" of engineers, many in the "new" materials of **iron**, **steel**, and **glass**, were being promoted as models for architecture. Adolf Loos declared engineers "our Greeks" and Le Corbusier espoused the virtues of the "Engineer's Aesthetic" in his seminal book *Vers une architecture*.

ABOVE: *In his design for the Amsterdam Stock Exchange (1896–1903), Hendrik Petrus Berlage aspired to derive its form from the logical use of the principal materials—brick, iron, and glass, with stone corbels and lintels.*

BELOW: *Viollet-le-Duc illustrated his lectures for his students with designs that reinterpreted the structural principles of Gothic architecture in terms of the possibilities opened up by iron.*

Understanding architecture as the "art of building" seems to derive from the French tradition and the recognition of the status of the medieval master masons. Despite the emergence of the artist-designer in the Renaissance, and the subsequent consolidation of the role of the professional architect, the distinction between "architecture" and "building" appears to have been of little concern before the interest in aesthetics and stylistic revivals of the nineteenth century.

This change in attitude had begun to set in during the eighteenth century when, in response to the wider distribution of wealth and growing feeling of individualism, the use of architectural ornament as a sign of social prestige led to the identification of mere "building" with cheapness—something that could be safely left to either trained artisans or practically minded engineers. Hence, a century later, James Fergusson's qualified enthusiasm for Joseph Paxton's Crystal Palace, which he felt lacked "a sufficient amount of decoration about its parts to take it entirely out of the category of first-class engineering and to make it entirely an object of fine art."

Despite the long-standing assumption that ornament was a necessary part of architecture, progressive architects and theorists such as A. W. N. Pugin in England and Eugène Emmanuel Viollet-le-Duc in France emphasized the importance of grounding design in clear, logical construction. The belief that the application of the laws of structure to the properties of materials would provide a new foundation for architectural form became central to the renewal of the view of architecture as the art of building. A notable model was provided by the Bauakademie—or school of architecture—completed by the leading German Neoclassicist, Karl Friedrich Schinkel, in Berlin in 1836. In place of the essay in the Classical style that might have been expected, Schinkel demonstrated his belief that utility was the first determinant of architecture. Instead of stone, he opted for brick, and throughout the building the dimensions were determined by the bonding pattern. The style was recognizably Classical, but every detail was rethought in terms of the properties of brick. The cornices had notably shallow projections; all the moldings were kept simple to avoid frost damage; and the segmental arches were reflected internally in shallow brick vaults tied with iron rods—as in the early English industrial buildings Schinkel had visited and admired.

By the time the fourth edition of Otto Wagner's book *Moderne Architektur* was published in 1914 it appeared under the title *Die Baukunst unserer Zeit*, (The Building Art of our Time). To his contemporaries, the new wording would have been an unequivocal sign that Wagner was aligning himself with those who believed that the future of architecture lay with the understanding of it as the art of building, not with the reworking of historical styles or innovations in ornamental detail. ∎

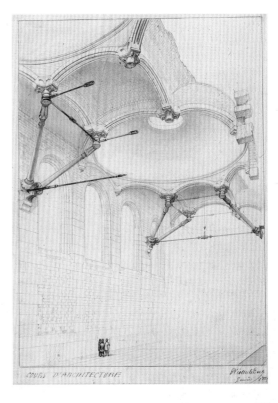

Architecture grounded in the means of construction

IDEA № 52

TECTONIC FORM

Derived from *tekton*, the Greek word for carpenter or builder, the term "tectonic" came into use in the mid-nineteenth century in the German-speaking world. Seeking to ground architecture in the crafts employed in its making, in a celebrated essay entitled "The Four Elements of Architecture" Gottfried Semper contrasted what he called the tectonic superstructure of wooden columns and roof with the stereotomic base of masonry.

To many architects this contrast between a light superstructure and a heavy, earthbound base epitomizes tectonic expression. It is seen, for example, in the juxtaposition of wood and brick in many domestic constructions, and on the grandest possible scale in the reflective, curved shells soaring above a rocklike platform at Sydney Opera House (1958–73), or in Mies van der Rohe's steel temple to modern art, the National Gallery in Berlin (1962–68).

Semper's usage of the term tectonic was derived from a highly influential account of Greek architecture by Karl Bötticher—*Die Tektonik der Hellenen*—which was published between 1843 and 1852. Bötticher stressed how all the parts of a Greek temple reinforced the overall architectural idea, and the word tectonic quickly assumed the broader meaning of a complete building system which bound all the elements into a structurally expressive aesthetic unity or form.

Although formulated in response to the simple trabeated structures of Greek architecture (those using a beamlike construction), the idea of tectonic form was generalized to signify an approach based on the "rational" expression of structure and construction, of which the **Gothic** as viewed by Pugin and Viollet-le-Duc presented an even more potent paradigm. Early Gothic structures, with their concentration of loads into points and lines of support, created a vivid impression of the play of structural forces. But whereas Greek temples, their columns apparently swelling under load, suggested a responsive acceptance of gravity, Gothic cathedrals soared in defiance of it, dissolving into a profusion of slender shafts and delicate traceries, leading Frank Lloyd Wright to accuse their masons of treating stone "as a negative material" with "neither limitations respected nor stone nature reinterpreted."

The emphasis on rational construction as the necessary corollary of tectonic expression was eventually attacked by August Schmarsow. Writing in 1893 in an essay entitled "The Essence of Architectural Creation" he argued that architects had much to gain by "disregarding... its entire execution in durable material" so as to rediscover its "time-honored inner aspect" as "the *creatress of space*." The emphasis on **space** as the essential "material" became central to Modernist architecture, but has recently been challenged by the influential critic Kenneth Frampton, whose 1992 book *Studies in Tectonic Culture* promoted renewed interest in the idea of tectonic expression. For Frampton, the all-too-fluid abstraction of space has been debased by the increasingly spectacular world of commercial building, and to oppose this he advocates regrounding architectural expression in the means of construction and **the nature of materials**. In this way, he hopes, architects might be able to resist the seemingly inexorable reduction of their art to **scenographic** effects. ■

The term "tectonic" came into use in
the nineteenth century when it was
frequently invoked to describe the
interrelationship between the outer
form and inner structure. Otto
Wagner's Karlsplatz Station in
Vienna (1899, opposite), with its clear
distinction between structure and
cladding exemplifies these ideas,
while Jørn Utzon's Bagsvaerd Church
(1974–76, main image), with its
framed exterior and concrete shell
ceiling, typifies the contemporary
understanding of "tectonic
expression" as construction
made manifest.

Buildings of many colors

IDEA № 53
POLYCHROMY

Few issues have divided architects and critics more than the use of color, and never more so than during the "polychrome war" that raged during the first half of the nineteenth century. It was sparked in 1815 by Quatremère de Quincy's book containing reconstructions of the colossal lost statues of Zeus and Athena by the great sculptor Phidias. Colored and studded with gold and ivory, they were an assault on the Neoclassical belief that the beauty of Greek art lay in abstract form.

"People of refinement," lamented Goethe in the early nineteenth century, "have a disinclination to colors." Half a century later, John Ruskin declared that "the pure and most thoughtful minds are those which love colour the most."

Fieldwork confirmed that Greek temples showed traces of applied color and following excavations in Selinus on Sicily, the Paris-based German architect, Jacques-Ignace Hittorff, made drawings of a conjectural reconstruction of a small temple resplendent in polychrome dress. The controversy it sparked spread across Europe. Many refused to believe the growing archaeological evidence, but for the color-loving Ruskin it became a matter of regret that the "temples whose azure and purple once flamed above the Grecian promontories" now "stand in their faded whiteness, like snow which the sunset has left cold."

The most far-reaching idea to come out of the debates about polychromy was developed by Gottfried Semper, who argued that Greek paint was a rarefied form of "dressing" or **cladding** that focused attention on the surface, not the material—an idea that became central to his conception of architectural **space**. Although Semper's ideas were to have a major long-term influence, the immediate impacts of the discovery of Greek polychromy were different. It undermined the growing rationalism of the day, which saw Greek temples as models of "logical" construction, acted as a stimulus to the Greek Revival, and contributed to the adoption of polychromy by advocates of the Gothic Revival, albeit as integral to the material, not as a decorative appliqué. Known as constructional or structural polychromy this also proved controversial; the work of its leading exponent, William Butterfield, was berated by some as "streaky bacon."

The widespread rejection of applied color reflected a growing sense of ease with the natural world and appreciation of the "natural" qualities of materials, so the fascination with polychromy proved short-lived. It was, however, renewed by Le Corbusier and other Modernists. The Berlin-based Bruno Taut argued that architects could offer people "an identification with their relatively modest living environment through the use of color"; and it was central to the work of the Dutch De Stijl movement, which adopted the chemist Wilhelm Ostwald's influential color theories without agreeing whether or not color was to be viewed symbolically or abstractly. Le Corbusier used colors to emphasize walls as planes, reinforcing or subverting the spatial and formal qualities. Characteristically, he developed a color system, basing it on pigments that were still made in roughly the same way as they had been throughout history. Invoking a musical analogy, he christened the harmonious combinations "color keyboards." ∎

Archaeological evidence that ancient Greek temples had been colored with paint fascinated a new generation of architects in the 1830s and 1840s, who made imaginative reconstructions (top) and used color in their own designs, as in Michael Gottlieb Bindesbøll's Thorvaldsen Museum in Copenhagen (1839–48, above).

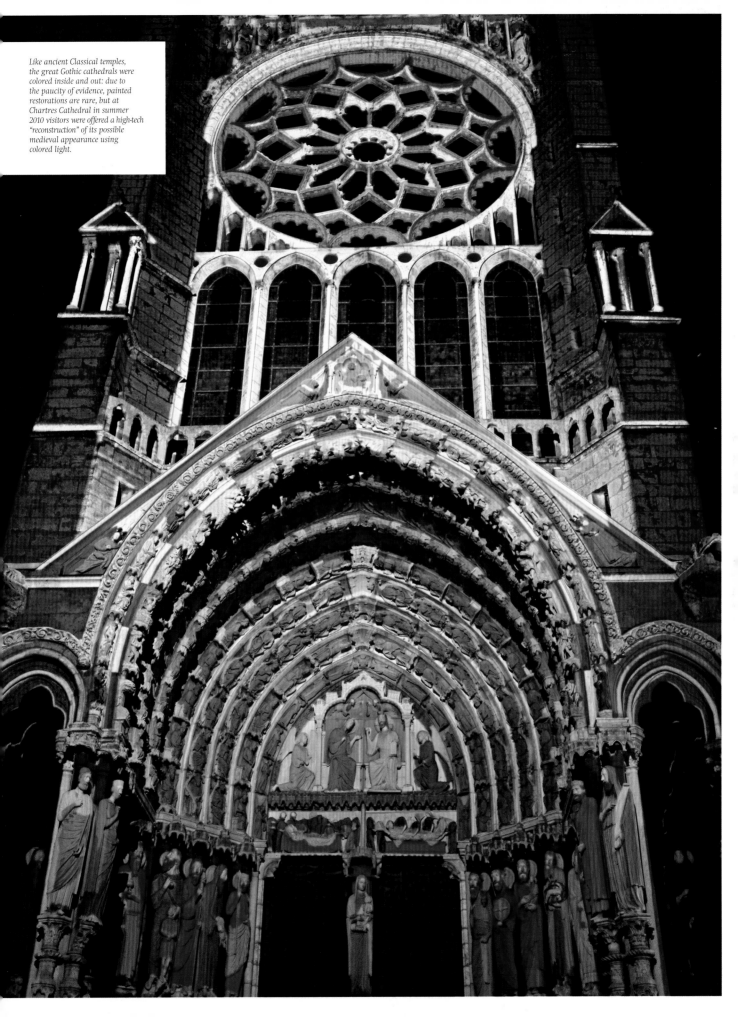

Like ancient Classical temples, the great Gothic cathedrals were colored inside and out: due to the paucity of evidence, painted restorations are rare, but at Chartres Cathedral in summer 2010 visitors were offered a high-tech "reconstruction" of its possible medieval appearance using colored light.

The walls of the fortified medieval town of Carcassonne were largely reconstructed by Viollet-le-Duc, an example—seen through the spectacles of today's practice—of "over enthusiastic" nineteenth-century conservation.

Saving it for the nation

IDEA № 54
CONSERVATION

Faced with the unprecedented rate of change initiated by the Industrial Revolution, the desire to preserve fine old buildings was widely felt in the nineteenth century. Preservation quickly turned into restoration—Eugène Emmanuel Viollet-le-Duc's reconstruction of Carcassonne (opposite) being among the largest—and in Britain increasingly zealous work on medieval churches prompted the formation of the Society for the Protection of Ancient Buildings (SPAB).

At the Castelvecchio in Verona, Carlo Scarpa developed an influential approach to conservation based on ensuring a clear distinction between old and new work. The latter was resolutely "modern" in character, as seen here in the cantilevered support that reinstates an equestrian statue to its former position.

In the founding manifesto of SPAB issued in 1877, William Morris, the leader of the Arts and Crafts movement, called for "Protection in the place of Restoration" and urged those responsible for the care of old buildings to "show no pretence of other art, and otherwise to resist all tampering with either the fabric or ornament of the building as it stands" and to accept that "modern art cannot meddle with-out destroying."

SPAB established a range of principles that are still widely followed. Favoring repair over restoration, it advocated regular maintenance and only work essential to a building's survival. Where new work was needed, it should be executed deferentially in sympathetic materials; an "honest alternative," not an attempt at reproduction. It stressed the importance of respecting the marks of time and understanding a building's integrity: the idea of gutting a building so that only the facade remained—a practice later encouraged by many planning authorities faced with the public unease provoked by many urban redevelopment projects—would not have been condoned.

In Britain, the National Trust for Places of Historic Interest or Natural Beauty was established in 1895 and has grown to become one of the country's most popular membership organizations, owning and/or managing hundreds of buildings, gardens, and landscapes. The first historic buildings law was passed in 1913 and in the 1920s a mysterious group of masked young women known as Ferguson's Gang opposed insensitive building and development and raised and donated money for the purchase of significant and threatened buildings. The 1944 Town and Country Planning Act introduced a national listing of historic buildings and five years later the National Trust for Historic Preservation was founded in the U.S.

In the face of large-scale redevelopment projects in the 1960s various *causes célèbres* acted as a focus for growing pubic concern about the loss of familiar landmarks. In January 1960 the British Transport Commission announced its intention to demolish Euston Station in London, including the massive Euston Arch built in 1837 in the Greek Revival style. The campaign for its preservation was led by an unlikely alliance of Victorian enthusiasts, including John Betjeman and Nikolaus Pevsner, and young Modernists such as Alison and Peter Smithson. Betjeman later campaigned successfully against the demolition of London's St. Pancras Station, while in the U.S. the demolition of New York's Pennsylvania Station in 1964 shocked the nation and lent weight to the preservation movement. The first postgraduate course in the subject, led by James Marston Fitch, began that year at Columbia University in New York and the scope of architectural conservation now embraces everything from ancient monuments to controversial Modernist buildings of the 1960s. ∎

The building as a projection of our feelings

IDEA № 55

EMPATHY

Empathy—or *Einfühlung* in German—is the idea that the vital properties we experience in, or attribute to, an object or another person are the projections of our own feelings and thoughts.

It was first elaborated by the German art psychologist Robert Vischer in his book *Das optische Formgefühl* (1872), and was adopted by such influential art historians as Heinrich Wölfflin and August Schmarsow, for whom the bodily encounter with a building was central to an understanding of the aesthetic experience of architecture.

The idea of *Einfühlung* had its roots in Immanuel Kant's assertion that pure beauty is the beauty of form. For some this was seen as a reaffirmation of the Platonic tradition of beauty as a product of mathematical relations; for others, notably the followers of Hegel, of a work of art's ability to express an Idea; and for the proponents of empathy theory, of their belief that beauty resided in the expression of feelings and emotions. Arguing that the dynamics of the formal relations in a work of art suggest equivalent muscular and emotional attitudes in the viewer, the last maintain that the viewer experiences those feelings as inherent qualities of the work. Aesthetic pleasure may therefore be explained as a form of self-enjoyment involving the fusion of subject and object.

Empathy theory was elaborated at considerable, and often confusing, length in Theodor Lipps's *Ästhetik*

(1903–06), and was introduced to a wide English audience by Geoffrey Scott in his 1924 book *The Architecture of Humanism*, in which he states: "Our aesthetic reactions are limited by our power to recreate in ourselves, imaginatively, the physical conditions suggested by the form we see: to ascribe its strength or weakness into terms of our own life." As its title suggests, Scott's book was a defense of Classicism; and one of the most commonly cited illustrations of our "power to recreate" was the *entasis* of Greek columns that made them appear, much as our bodies might, to swell and "flex their muscles" under load. Our inability to relate in this way to some "new" materials was pointed out by the German architect Adolf Göller (1846–1902) who argued that we perceive iron columns to be flimsy, just as we perceive a stork's legs to be too thin, because "we imagine ourselves standing on such legs and feel ourselves in a very precarious equilibrium."

As the titles of their best-known works indicate, the bodily, non-intellectual experience of architecture was emphasized by two influential Scandinavian writers on architecture: Steen Eiler Rasmussen, whose 1959 book *Experiencing Architecture* is still

TOP: *Cast-iron columns, such as these in a flax-spinning mill (Shrewsbury, England, 1796) struck many early observers, familiar with proportions based on stone, as uncomfortably slender.*

ABOVE: *The "flowing" lowest stair and flexing steel balusters of this stair in Gunnar Asplund's Law Courts Extension in Gothenburg (1934–38) are designed to suggest that they are responding to the user's presence.*

widely recommended in schools of architecture, and Christian Norberg-Schulz, whose *Experience, Time and Architecture* (1963) was intended as a counter to the more abstract aspects of architecture emphasized by Sigfried Giedion in his seminal *Space, Time and Architecture* (1941). More recently, an emphasis on sensual qualities has been central to architectural theory and practice grounded in **phenomenology** as articulated in the writings of Martin Heidegger, Maurice Merleau-Ponty, and others, and in Tadao Ando's exploration of the Japanese idea of *shintai*, which emphasizes unity between man and nature. ■

The entasis *(swelling profile) of Doric columns such as these early examples at the Temple of Ceres at Paestum (late sixth century* BC*) have been widely interpreted as appearing to swell, like the muscles of our bodies, under load.*

IDEA № 56
AIR CONDITIONING

Air-conditioning systems, as opposed to **central heating** and ventilation, can cool as well as warm buildings. Their antecedents lie in traditional techniques, from the use of cool water from aqueducts in ancient Rome and early rotary fans in China, to exploiting the evaporation of water in the Middle East. As early as the 1600s, James I of England was treated to a demonstration of "turning Summer into Winter" by Cornelius Drebbel. It involved the addition of salt to water, but the invention of air conditioning proper stems from nineteenth- and early twentieth-century discoveries and inventions.

In 1820, Michael Faraday found that the compression and liquefaction of ammonia would dramatically cool air when the liquid gas was allowed to evaporate, and in 1842 in Florida the physician John Gorrie used compressors to create ice for cooling hospital patients. He had the vision of a centralized air-conditioning system for cooling whole cities but the idea died with his financial backer. A similarly visionary proposition was suggested by the Expressionist poet Paul Scheerbart, who thought of cooled air flowing between layers of glass, like the "neutralizing walls" proposed by Le Corbusier—possibly with a debt to Scheerbart—in the late 1920s.

The first electrical air-conditioning system was invented in 1902 by Willis Haviland Carrier. His "Apparatus for Treating Air" controlled temperature and humidity in a printworks in Brooklyn, New York, and the resulting increase in productivity led to the formation of the Carrier Air Conditioning Company of America, which introduced the first mass-produced domestic system—called the Weathermaker—in 1928. Fitted individually to windows, such unit air conditioners would become a familiar feature of American homes.

Although air conditioning was invaluable in many specialist building types such as museums and art galleries, laboratories, and hospitals, and in hot and humid climates, like **electric lighting** its broader architectural impact was far from benign. Beyond the challenge of accommodating large ducts, which led Louis Kahn to declare "it was easy for Ledoux—no pipes" and to develop the idea of **servant and served spaces**, the growing dependence on energy-demanding mechanical systems enabled architects to neglect issues of orientation and window design that could both reduce energy costs and promote architectural character. The belief in a "perfect" regime of light, temperature, and humidity for offices also led to increasingly homogenized environments.

Later developments enabled localized user-control of environmental conditions and, as the implications of the energy crisis of the early 1970s sank in, architects began to rediscover **passive design** techniques for reducing or eliminating dependence on air conditioning. In hot, oil-rich countries, however, it continues to find exotic new uses: Dubai has acquired an indoor ski slope, and more than

Building services such as air conditioning demand a considerable amount of money and space. Rather than conceal them in ducts, in the
Pompidou Center in Paris Renzo Piano and Richard Rogers opted to let them dominate the building's street elevation.

500 air-conditioned bus shelters are planned as part of the new infrastructure of Abu Dhabi. Faced with the potentially extreme impacts of global warming, energy-intensive "climate fortresses" have even been suggested as a means of securing the thermal comfort of wealthy individuals and significant institutions. ∎

es in inhospitable
...ubai, would be
...air conditioning.

The end of ornament

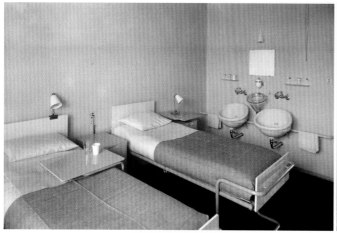

ABOVE LEFT: *The patients at Paimio Sanatorium shared double rooms in which every detail was rethought: from glare-free lighting to radiant overhead heating, splash-free basins to steel-framed beds raised to facilitate cleaning.*

ABOVE RIGHT: *The flat roof of the sanatorium was used as a continuous deck for the patients to experience fresh air and sun—then the only "cure" for tuberculosis.*

IDEA № 57

FORM FOLLOWS FUNCTION

Few debates in architectural theory have been as vexed as those around the interrelationships of the Vitruvian triad of **commodity, firmness, and delight**. Arguing that "form follows function," advocates of Functionalism believe that "delight"—or beauty—is the inevitable consequence of paying proper attention to the functional and structural requirements of a building.

This idea has its roots among Gothic-Revival architects such as A. W. N. Pugin and Eugène Emmanuel Viollet-le-Duc. Arguing that there should be "no features about a building which are not necessary for convenience, construction, or propriety," Pugin believed that "all ornament should consist of enrichment of the essential construction of the building." This view was echoed in the U.S. by Louis Sullivan, who coined the phrase "form (ever) follows function" and illustrated it by reference to natural examples such as an eagle in flight, a flowering blossom, and a flowing stream— precisely the kind of biological analogy that would soon become common.

As a master of intricate, organically inspired ornament that at times threat- ened to engulf his forms, Sullivan's view of a "functional" architecture was clearly different to Pugin's, and "form follows function" begs the questions "which" and "whose" functions are to be followed? For some, **ornament** such as the **Classical Orders**, is one of the defining "functions" of architecture. To the Modernists, however, in tune with Adolf Loos' declaration that "**ornament is crime**," its elimination was seen as a necessary cleansing.

As a slogan to describe the approach of architects seeking to come to terms with the demands of new social needs and technological means, however, "form follows function" served well, and in specialized buildings such as the Paimio Sanatorium (1928–33, above and opposite) by Alvar Aalto,

"No features about a building which are not necessary for convenience, construction, or propriety."

Functionalist ideals inspired everything from the zoning of the plan to innovative fittings and furniture. A widely accepted feature of Functionalist architecture was the expression of structure. But this was not straightforward: Mies van der Rohe, for example, whose "skin and bones" designs purported to be expressions of their **structural frames**, so disliked the cross-bracing needed for stability that it was rarely expressed. Similarly, although Le Corbusier's declaration that "the house is a machine for living in" might seem a classic statement of a Functionalist view, his work hardly bears that out. The **free plan** was a brilliant response to more relaxed modern lifestyles, but its architectural expression did not follow as an inevitable consequence of them, and another of the key points of Le Corbusier's **Five Points of a New Architecture**, the ribbon window, was not as "functional" as some traditional types.

In the 1930s, with the coining of the term "**International Style**," the architecture of "form follows function" became increasingly identified with a stripped-down, ornament-free approach to design as a form of aesthetic packaging rather than inventive problem-solving. It is the ultimate irony of this fraught idea that many of the "Functionalist" buildings that spread around the world proved, in terms of their occupants' needs and environmental performance, to be among the most dysfunctional ever built. ∎

Assembled from functionally defined wings, Alvar Aalto's Paimio Sanatorium (1928–33) offered, from overall organization to detail and furniture, an unusually thorough application of the principle "form follows function."

Through its teaching and building, the Bauhaus school of architecture and design, built in Dessau to designs by its director Walter Gropius in 1926, did more than any other institution to give tangible form to the spirit of the Machine Age.

"Architecture is the will of an epoch translated into space; living, changing, new."

Spirit of the age

IDEA № 58
ZEITGEIST

In 1828 a little-known German architect, Heinrich Hübsch, published a book *In Which Style Should We Build?* His question was echoed later by the leading Neoclassicist, Karl Friedrich Schinkel: "Every major period has left behind its own style of architecture. Why should we not try to find a style for ourselves?" Therein lay an idea that was to prove hugely influential in the formation of the Modern Movement in architecture, that of the Zeitgeist or "Spirit of the Age."

The elegant geometric forms of this lamp (above, designed by Marianne Brandt and Hans Przyrembel in 1926) and of Marcel Breuer's influential Wassily Chair (1925–27, below) are typical of the Bauhaus style whose influence is still felt.

The German architect Peter Behrens for example, sought "an absolute clarification of spatial form to mathematical precision" as an expression of the German "folk spirit," while in the early 1920s Mies van der Rohe declared that "architecture is the will of an epoch translated into **space**; living, changing, new."

This idea has deep roots in German philosophy. To Immanuel Kant, history was the unfolding of a "world plan" in which each age finds its natural expression, while for Hegel the Zeitgeist was an active force shaping the ethos of a particular society or civilization and defining their position in the sociocultural progression of humanity. This view of history exerted a formative influence on the German-speaking founders of academic art history—Jacob Burckhardt, Heinrich Wölfflin, Alois Riegl, and Erwin Panofsky, among others—and through them two of the leading promoters of Modern architecture, Nikolaus Pevsner and Sigfried Giedion. In his book *Space, Time and Architecture*, published in 1941, the latter wrote that it was through Wölfflin that he had "learned to grasp the spirit of an epoch."

For proponents of what Pevsner christened the Modern Movement the elusive spirit of the times was to be found in the efficiency of the machine and the inevitable replacement of craftwork by mass production—hence the frequent use of the phrase Machine Age, and the belief that the representative new architecture would emerge from the rational use of new materials such as **steel**, **reinforced concrete**, and plate **glass**. In promoting this view Pevsner, Giedion, and others constructed histories of Modern architecture that traced an inexorable line of development from the Gothic Revival, with its emphasis on construction as the basis of architecture, via the Arts and Crafts movement and art nouveau, to what became known as the **International Style**. First presented in 1936 in Pevsner's book *Pioneers of the Modern Movement* (expanded and republished in 1949 as *Pioneers of Modern Design*) this view continues to echo through histories of the period.

The idea of the Zeitgeist as an active force shaping architecture was widely criticized by **Postmodernists**, and the most concerted assault came in 1977 with the publication of David Watkin's book *Morality and Architecture*. As a champion of Classicism, Watkin found the Modernist rejection of all other styles as out of tune with "the times" irksome, and he loathed the moralistic attitude that he traced through A. W. Pugin, Eugène Emmanuel Viollet-le-Duc, Le Corbusier, and others who claimed their chosen style was the only one that was truthful and rational, reflecting society's real needs. ∎

The fundamental architectural "material"

IDEA № 59
SPACE

The idea that space is the primary "material" of architecture pervades the literature of Modernism and architectural history, yet is of surprisingly recent origin. It probably dates to 1893 and the inaugural lecture of August Schmarsow as chair of art history at Leipzig University.

Entitled "The Essence of Architectural Creation," Schmarsow's presentation attacked the idea that the essence of architecture lay in the **tectonic** assembly of elements of construction, proposing instead that it must be found in a larger conception of the whole. Describing his theory as "genetic," he grounded it in human psychology: "Our sense of space and spatial imagination press toward spatial creation; they seek their satisfaction in art. We call this art architecture; in plain words, it is the creatress of space."

In keeping with the German preoccupation with the idea of the Zeitgeist, Schmarsow also argued that the source of spatial conceptions would be found in the "innermost energies of the culture." In this he drew on the ideas of Alois Riegl, who wrote about an era's *Kunstwollen* or "will to art." To advocates of a new architecture for the Machine Age this idea held an obvious appeal and among the first to apply it was Peter Behrens, in whose office three key figures of Modern architecture—Mies van der Rohe, Le Corbusier, and Walter Gropius—worked.

Schmarsow's assertion of the pre-eminence of space quickly caught hold among art historians, critics, and architects. Geoffrey Scott, the English defender of Renaissance **humanism**, for example, wrote that "the architect models in space as a sculptor in clay. He designs his space as a work of art." But it fell to Sigfried Giedion, with his 1941 book *Space, Time and Architecture*, to popularize the idea that the essence of Modern architecture lay in the development of a new "space conception" based on the "interpenetration" of interior and exterior into a spatial

MAIN IMAGE: *Set amid the symmetrical composition of Classical buildings of the 1929 Barcelona International Exposition, few if any buildings have better expressed the Modernist vision of space—"flowing," dynamic, asymmetrical—than Mies van der Rohe's Barcelona Pavilion.*

OPPOSITE: *In his Willemspark School (1980–83) Herman Hertzberger combines spatial continuity with a richly inhabitable interior to create a perfect setting for the school's educational ideals.*

"We call this art architecture; in plain words, it is the creatress of space."

continuum. Frank Lloyd Wright had posited something similar in the early years of the century in his vision of an extensive "prairie space," while in the 1920s the De Stijl group's Neoplasticist space, Le Corbusier's idea of an *espace indicible* (ineffable space), and various other inflections of the same core idea competed as expressions of the new age. No one put these widely shared aspirations more clearly than Mies van der Rohe, who wrote in 1923 that "architecture is the will of an epoch translated into **space**; living, changing, new."

Although the abstract quality of Modernist space was "softened" by many of the second generation of Modern architects, such as Alvar Aalto, and challenged by Aldo van Eyck, who advocated "**place** and occasion" over the abstractions of "space and time," the idea that creation of space is the primary task of architecture remains central to most thinking. Nowhere is this truer than in the "warped spaces" of Frank Gehry, Daniel Libeskind, and a new generation of digital designers in which some see the emerging expression of our own **Zeitgeist**. ∎

The shock of the new

IDEA № 60
MODERNITY

Modernity in architecture emerged from artistic movements in the second decade of the twentieth century and reflected the era's technical innovations. It was defined by a concern for abstraction, space, and transparency.

This photographic montage by the Russian artist El Lissitzky (1890–1941) combines two iconic images of Modernity—what Le Corbusier called the type sportif, *and the electrographic townscape of the industrial city.*

"By modernity," wrote the poet Charles Baudelaire in a celebrated essay entitled "The Painter of Modern Life" published in 1863, "I mean the ephemeral, the contingent, the half of art whose other half is eternal and immutable." The sense of modernity Baudelaire described was perhaps first manifested visually in Impressionist paintings—in scenes of the bustling life of the fashionable new boulevards of Haussmann's Paris or the fleeting effects of light on water or foliage—and it came in time to characterize a series of interrelated movements across Europe such as Fauvism and Expressionism, Cubism and Futurism, Dadaism and Surrealism, that flourished in the years either side of the First World War. And while architecture, as the art of the relatively stable, long-term business of building, might be thought necessarily to tend toward the "eternal and immutable," architects were equally eager to capture in their work the modernity of the industrial city.

The first architect to link the words "Modern" and "Architecture" in print was Otto Wagner in Vienna. Together they formed the title of an 1896 book based on his inaugural lecture as Professor of Architecture at the city's Academy of Fine Art. Arguing that architecture should reflect the fact that "new human tasks and views called for a change or reconstitution of existing forms" he called for bright, well-ventilated houses with simple furnishings in harmony with "the checkered breeches" and other leisure clothes seen in the modern city, and advocated the use of thin slabs of stone cladding as an "honest" expression of new forms of construction using a structural frame.

Celebrating the potential of new ways of building became central to the expression of modernity in architecture, so much so that Wagner retitled the final edition of his book *Die Baukunst unserer Zeit* ("The Building Art of Our Time") to align himself unmistakably with progressive trends. The full expression of modernity in architecture, as in the other visual arts, involved a series of aesthetic and technical innovations. **Abstraction** provided a means of stripping away outdated stylistic forms and reducing a building to a language of "pure" form. The shallow **layering** of **space** in Cubism found an echo in the free plans of Le Corbusier's 1920s villas. Large sheets of plate glass offered both the **transparency** that allowed spatial continuity and the expression of structure, and also a beguiling play of reflections that could capture the ephemeral and contingent qualities of the modern city identified by Baudelaire—in his two projects for Glass Towers of 1919 (opposite) and 1923 Mies van der Rohe attempted to exploit reflections through, respectively, a faceted and undulating plan. Finally, building forms could evoke more dynamic and advanced technologies, such as ocean liners and motor cars. Erich Mendelsohn's Einstein Tower (see p.142) was perhaps the first building to look as if it might be moving through space rather than stably occupying it, and Le Corbusier's houses, following his **Five Points of a New Architecture**, were poised lightly on *pilotis*, making them seem only half-attached to their sites while their roof gardens evoked the feeling of being on a ship's deck. ∎

Mies van der Rohe's rendering of his 1919 competition project for a glass skyscraper on Berlin's Friedrichstrasse fused the "Functionalist" belief in constructional "honesty"—the inner structure is clearly visible—with an Expressionist fascination with the fugitive play of reflections.

For Frank Lloyd Wright the "nature" of concrete lay in its fluidity, an idea that eventually found dramatic expression in the helical forms of the Guggenheim Museum (1943–58) in New York.

BELOW: *Clad with tiny wooden shingles outside and framed and furnished with wood internally, Peter Zumthor's Saint Benedict Chapel (1989) in the Graubünden region of Switzerland exemplifies the aesthetic advantages of working primarily with a single material.*

IDEA № 61

IN THE NATURE OF MATERIALS

"Every new material," declared Frank Lloyd Wright, "means a new form, a new use if used according to its nature." The belief that working "in the nature of materials" could be the hallmark of an authentically *modern* architecture grew out of nineteenth-century debates about **style**, but its roots lie in the emergence of modern science.

Both Galileo and Leonardo da Vinci realized that structures could not simply be scaled up and down in size, but that their proportions had to change according to their size and materials—as was the case, Galileo pointed out, with animal skeletons. The Classical view that forms were independent of matter was no longer tenable, and scientists and engineers began to quantify the properties of materials to enable their performance to be calculated mathematically.

The belief that the application of the laws of structure to the properties of materials would provide a new foundation for architectural form became central to the view of architecture as the **art of building**. The most systematic development of this constructional rationalism was articulated in France by Viollet-le-Duc, who argued that a thorough knowledge of materials is "the first condition of composition," and that architects would "proceed as Nature herself does."

Expressing the "nature" of a material, however, is not as straightforward in practice as it might appear in theory. Louis Kahn could ask a brick "what it wanted" if he needed to make an opening in a wall and receive the reply "I like an arch," but with many materials the answers were not so clear. It is the "nature" of glass to be both transparent and, for those hoping it will reveal the structure within,

annoyingly reflective—a quality which may, however, be valued, as in the work of Swiss architects such as Peter Zumthor and Gigon Guyer.

With a composite material such as **reinforced concrete** things become more difficult. Its strength depends on hidden steel bars and meshes; its final appearance is determined by the "nature" of the material in which it is cast more than its own composition; it is fluid while being poured, solid when set. Wright's Guggenheim Museum (opposite) is a monument to the fluidity of concrete, whereas in the slab over the concourse of Sydney Opera House (see p.39) Jørn Utzon exploited the same property to create a structure that appears as accurate to the forces at work in it as the bones in our bodies.

Like all attempts to ground architectural forms in some absolute determinant, such as function or structure, working "in the nature of materials" does not offer a simple route to a "logical" solution. Rather, it describes an attitude that seeks to allow form to develop in response to a range of **particular** conditions, in contrast to one imposed through the adoption of a preexisting **style**.

"The fabriclike quality of hanging carpets and cloths recalled by modern construction."

Like many of their buildings, Herzog and de Meuron's Laban Dance Centre (1997–2002) in east London reveals their continuing fascination with the potential of cladding a building with variously opaque, translucent, and transparent materials.

Well-dressed walls

CLADDING

The idea of cladding is ancient: the Greeks painted their marble and the Romans generally "dressed" brick walls with a thin revetment of stone. But in the nineteenth century it became the subject of heated debate. A catalyst was the emergence of the **structural frame** and the reduction of a building's enclosing walls to a non-load-bearing envelope. What should be the basis for the architectural expression of this new way of building?

Photographed under construction in 1992 in Philadelphia, this high-rise tower reveals the "freedom" of modern construction: a standardized steel frame supports cladding rails and panels that need bear no relation to the underlying construction.

Practically, the most exhilarating answers emerged in late nineteenth-century Chicago as architects came to grips with buildings of unprecedented height. Burnham and Root's Reliance Building (1890–95), for example, consisted of successive ribbons of plate glass, anticipating the development of the curtain wall. The foundations for a theory of cladding, however, were prompted by a seemingly arcane debate about archaeologists' discovery that Greek temples were originally painted in bright colors, not "pure" marble constructions (see pp.112–13).

To many this was anathema, but to the German architect Gottfried Semper it confirmed the Greeks' refined aesthetic sense. Semper's ideas crystallized around a Caribbean hut shown at the Great Exhibition of 1851 in London and were articulated in an essay entitled "The Four Elements of Architecture." If the essence of architecture was the enclosure of space, he argued, and the original space-defining elements were not structural walls but carpets and cloths hung from a frame, then their fabric-like quality should be recalled by modern construction.

Semper's theories proved widely influential. The buildings of the Viennese architect Otto Wagner emulated them directly: his Majolica House (1898–99) was clad with tiles that created a vast floral "fabric" that appeared to hang from giant studs, while the surface of his Post Office Savings Bank (1894–1902) was marked by the fixings for its manifestly thin stone cladding—an approach that another advocate of architectural "honesty," the English critic John Ruskin, would have approved: in *Stones of Venice* he praised the "confessed rivets" used to fix thin panels of stone to the walls of St. Mark's Basilica.

Adolf Loos' 1898 article "The Principle of Cladding" offered an elaboration of Semper's ideas, and in his work Loos provided vivid examples of how to implement what he called the "language of forms" implicit in materials. Externally, he favored either a coat of render or thin, highly figured stones that were manifestly not structural (he called them "permanent wallpaper"); internally he selected materials according to a room's purpose and mood—in the Villa Müller in Prague (1930, see p.134), for example, the ladies' reading room is finished in light wood veneers, the library in more "masculine" dark mahogany.

The curtain walls developed in Chicago have long been seen as central to the development of Modern architecture and it is only recently that Semper's ideas have been reexamined, leading to provocative rereadings of the early work of Le Corbusier as a "pure" white dressing of raw construction, and to widespread interest in the material surfaces of buildings. Associated initially with the work of leading Swiss architects such as Herzog and de Meuron (opposite) and Peter Zumthor, this is now almost universal, partly in response to a recent, far-reaching technical innovation, **rainscreen cladding**. ■

Architecture emulating biological forms

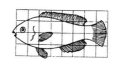

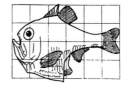
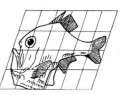
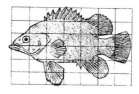
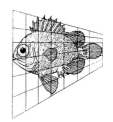

ORGANIC ARCHITECTURE

A work of architecture can be understood as possessing inner "laws"—of geometry, structure, **proportion**, and so on—that are conditioned by the specific circumstances of the choice of materials and site. This is analogous to an organism, which responds to both its inner constitution and its external circumstances.

In his classic book On Growth and Form *(1917) D'Arcy Wentworth Thompson argued that biologists overemphasized evolution at the expense of physical laws and mechanics. Evocative illustrations such as these geometric transformations of fishes helped ensure his influence on several generations of designers.*

The idea that a work of art is analagous to a natural organism in its interdependence of parts to form a whole goes back to Aristotle's *Poetics* and gained new momentum in German thought in the eighteenth and nineteenth centuries, playing a vital role in the ideas of Kant and Hegel, and preoccupying Goethe. Drawing on his studies of plants, Goethe proposed two aspects to their formation: the law of inner nature, according to which the organism is constituted, and the law of outer circumstances, by which it is modified by the environment.

Goethe's ideas had a major impact on Frank Lloyd Wright, who professed a more thoroughgoing commitment to creating an "organic" architecture than any major architect. His use of the term was, however, both all-embracing —involving the response to site, working "in the nature of materials" and, frequently, a pervasive grid or module—and exclusive: no one else's work, in Wright's view, was truly organic.

The advent of evolutionary thought encouraged the idea that architectural styles could "evolve" like natural organisms, while biologists increasingly looked at natural forms as being the result of both a functional fitness-for-purpose and underlying morphological rules, such as the seemingly ubiquitous logarithmic spiral, or "curve of life" as it was sometimes called. This latter strand of thinking culminated with the publication in 1917 of D'Arcy Wentworth Thompson's magisterial book *On Growth and Form*. Although out of tune with the biology of its time, it eventually enjoyed enormous popularity among architects—it was the only book that the architect of Sydney Opera House, Jørn Utzon, asked his staff to read—and has recently found new favor with exponents of complexity theory.

The Functionalist strand of thought was popularized in the 1920s by the German biologist Raoul Francé. In a short book entitled *Plants as Inventors* (published in German in 1923, and in English in 1926), Francé wrote that "necessity prescribes certain forms for certain qualities. Therefore it is always possible... to infer the activity from the shape, the purpose from the form. In nature all forms... are a creation of necessity." The parallels with Functionalist thinking in architecture are obvious and Francé's illustrations found their way into books by leading Modernists, not least those of Le Corbusier who declared biology "the great new word in architecture and planning."

With the advent of form-generating software, designing buildings in a manner analogous to the way nature creates organisms has gained new momentum. Proponents of "evolutionary architecture" such as the American Greg Lynn see it as a form of artificial life, subject to similar principles of morphogenesis, genetic coding, replication, and selection, and aim to make buildings capable of the symbiotic behavior and metabolic balance that are characteristic of natural organisms. To date, most of this work can only be experienced in simulations, but it stands in an ancient lineage. ∎

"In Nature all forms... are a creation of necessity."

The Spanish architect-engineer Santiago Calatrava frequently claims inspiration from nature, as seen here in the Quadracci Pavilion, a major addition to Milwaukee Art Museum completed in 2001. The fully glazed reception hall is surmounted by an adjustable, winglike sunscreen (above), while the galleria (right) is said to have been inspired by a wave, and to resemble the bleached bones of a shark.

The austere exteriors of Adolf Loos's houses, such as here at the Villa Müller in Prague (1930), epitomize the ideas expressed in his 1908 essay "Ornament and Crime." The exterior is, however, in striking contrast to its richly decorated interior.

Declaring the "truth" of modern construction

IDEA № 64

ORNAMENT IS CRIME

The phrase "ornament is crime" emanates from a 1908 essay by Adolf Loos. In it he argued that the contemporary use of ornament on buildings, furniture, clothes, and other everyday things was a means of masking the mediocrity of the culture.

Completed in 1911 on the Michaelerplatz in Vienna the mixed-use Looshaus has large areas of richly figured marble which Adolf Loos, following Otto Wagner's lead, regarded as a substitute for traditional craftsmanship.

The essay was not widely available in print until 1920, when it appeared in Paris in the second issue of the magazine *L'Esprit Nouveau*, founded by Le Corbusier and the painter Amedée Ozenfant. Loos did not, in fact, identify crime with ornament in such a blatant manner as "ornament is crime" suggests: he believed that *"cultural evolution is equivalent to the removal of ornament from articles in daily use"*—the only phrase he italicized; his title was "Ornament and Crime"; and his immediate target the ornamental excesses of the Vienna Secession.

Loos's essay owes its notoriety partly to his colorful style of argument. He compared the tattooing of Papuans, which he saw as the beginning of art, with the tattooing of modern men, a mark of criminal degeneracy. Despite his opposition to ornament, the highly figured stones and richly veined woods in his own work confirm that he was not against decoration, which he understood as part of a set of conventions to convey meaning and status within a shared social order.

The real crime, in Loos's view, was that ornamenting functional objects embroiled them in the ephemeral world of fashion: ornament was proper for decorative fabrics or carpets, whose life was limited, but it was an insult to well-designed buildings and objects made of durable materials. In part his argument was aesthetic—he had, he declared, a "passion for smooth and precious surfaces"—but it was also evolutionary and moral: he saw the elimination of ornament as a biological

fact, and hated the waste of resources that condemned well-made things to go out of fashion.

Looking back in 1924 on the notoriety his essay had by then achieved, Loos wrote that he "never thought like the purists who took this reasoning to the absurd, that ornament should be systematically abolished. It is only where the passage of time makes it disappear that it cannot be reborn." But it was too late: lack of ornament was a hallmark of the new architecture, equated with honesty and simplicity, and would be declared a defining feature of the **International Style**.

The phrase "ornament is crime" was destined to become a watchword of the new style's supposed moral purity and a stick with which to beat deviants. It was only with the arrival of

Postmodernism in the 1970s that the virtues of ornament were again seriously advocated—albeit initially as an ironic form of commentary on the shortcomings of **Modernism** rather than as part of a coherent view of a more inclusive architecture. Perhaps the ultimate irony attending the recent history of **ornament** is that having been expunged in the search for an expression of the Machine Age, the resurgence of interest stems in part from the capabilities of **computer-aided design**. ■

The open, flowing interior

BELOW: *Composed of freely arranged planes of fine stones and clear and colored glass, Mies van der Rohe's Barcelona Pavilion, designed for the 1929 International Exposition, epitomized the new ideal of the free plan. See pp.124–25 for photograph.*

OPPOSITE: *The open plan of Gerrit Rietveld's Schröder House (1924) could be transformed by sliding walls to create private spaces for Mrs. Schröder and her children.*

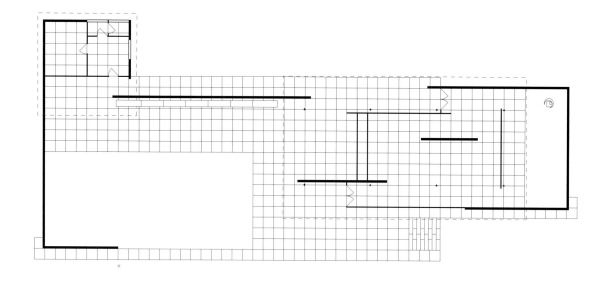

IDEA Nº 65

FREE PLAN

The "free plan" or *plan libre* arose out of the convergence of two ideas: structural frames of **steel** or **concrete** that freed internal subdivisions of their traditional load-bearing function, and the opening up of spatial composition.

It began in the English Arts and Crafts movement and crystallized with Frank Lloyd Wright's "destruction of the box" in his Prairie-style houses of the early twentieth century. The *plan libre* was also the third of the **Five Points of a New Architecture** published by Le Corbusier in 1927 to promote his ideas at the Weissenhof in Stuttgart, a demonstration housing development featuring the work of Europe's leading Modern architects.

Le Corbusier's expression of the free plan was characterized by the counterpoint between the structural grid and partition walls that demonstrated their freedom from

structural constraint by sliding past columns and wrapping around such secondary features as baths and washbasins. In the Villa Savoye (1928–30, see p.141), the culminating achievement of this phase of his work, a central ramp rose through the now fluid space from inside to out, and the staircase stood free as a sculptural form bathed in light.

Although associated with Le Corbusier, the open, "flowing" space of the free plan was central to the work of all the leading Modernist architects. The Dutch exponents of the De Stijl movement made less of the structural grid, preferring—as in Gerrit Rietveldt's

Schröder House of 1924 (opposite)—to compose with colored planes. Mies van der Rohe's exploration of spatial fluidity culminated in two spatial types: the undifferentiated, gridded space of his projects for glass skyscrapers of 1919 (see p.127) and 1923, and the planar composition of freestanding walls that characterized his Brick Villa of 1923. These systems were combined in the seminal Barcelona Pavilion of 1929 (above and pp.124–25), a composition of cruciform, chrome-clad columns and planes of richly figured stone and clear and colored glass, which many saw as the definitive expression of the Modernist vision of space.

Although he later used numerous other compositional and constructional systems, Le Corbusier continued to explore the potential of the free plan throughout his career, deploying it to brilliant effect in such large-scale designs as the Assembly Building in Chandigarh, India. Mies, on the other hand, pushed it further by proposing the idea of a column-free "universal space" to be deployed at every scale from the house to major public buildings such as the 164ft- (50m-) square pavilion for the National Gallery in Berlin (1962–68). In the Farnsworth House (1945–51, p.154), the floating floor and roof planes were supported by six I-section steel columns and the open space was articulated, but not subdivided, by a service core containing bathrooms and kitchen equipment and storage.

The spatial possibilities of the free plan continue to fascinate architects: Rem Koolhaas, for example, has extended the potential of the Villa Savoye ramp by developing the floors of public buildings as a continuous surface, while Mies's universal space has been applied commercially, first in the idea of *bürolandschaft* or "office landscape" and latterly, and more prosaically, in the increasingly ubiquitous separation between "shell and core" structure and circulation, and the "fit-out" to suit a particular occupant. ∎

A journey through a building

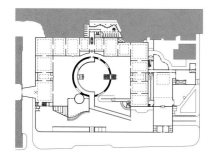

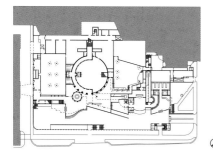

IDEA Nº 66

ARCHITECTURAL PROMENADE

Introducing the Villa Savoye in the second volume of his *Œuvre Complète*, Le Corbusier explained that "we are dealing with a true architectural promenade offering constantly varied, unexpected, sometimes astonishing aspects."

These qualities could also, as he pointed out in *Vers une architecture*, be encountered on that bastion of Classicism, the Athenian Acropolis, and were the antithesis of the axial symmetry and stiff formality of French **Beaux-Arts** architecture. It was in opposition to the similarly axial organization of the garden style perfected by André Le Nôtre in seventeenth-century France that the precursor of the architectural promenade crystallized: in the landscaped or, later, **Picturesque** gardens of eighteenth-century England, whose designers aimed to stimulate visitors by offering varying, unexpected sensations and ever changing views.

Fascinated by the experiential possibilities of the architectural promenade, Le Corbusier sought to juxtapose the clear spatial order established by the column grid and floor slabs—explained in the **Five Points of a New Architecture**—with the free movement of people through it. Ramps extended the journey between floors, while stairs were presented as sculptural elements in space that both enabled and represented vertical movement through the building. Both qualities are apparent in the second unbuilt project for a house for a certain Madame Meyer: Le Corbusier presented,

BELOW: *Made popular by Le Corbusier, the idea of an architectural promenade through a building has found few more compelling expressions than in the external public route that forms an armature of Stirling Wilford's extension of the Staatsgalerie in* *Stuttgart (1977–83). Connecting two streets and negotiating a difference in height of some 49ft (15m), the route takes people around the inner edge of the drum that forms the focus of the extension (see plans opposite below).*

"Constantly varied, unexpected, sometimes astonishing aspects."

as sketches in a letter, the sequence of vistas it would offer as she walked from the main living room to a culminating view toward a Picturesque ruin.

Following the Second World War the Picturesque garden was invoked as a model for an approach to urban design. Christened "Townscape" by the editors of the *Architectural Review*, its most persuasive advocate, Gordon Cullen, emphasized the experiential qualities of towns and proposed "Serial Vision," a town-scale version of the architectural promenade, as a guiding principle.

Among contemporary architects, Rem Koolhaas has extended the Corbusian version of the architectural promenade by transforming the floor plates and ramps into a continuous public realm comprised of large horizontal and sloping planes. To emphasize the resulting spatial continuity he frequently presents his

projects using unfolded sections that describe the complex spatial journey as a linear route. The Portuguese architect Alvaro Siza, on the other hand, is preoccupied by particular moments of perception. The drawings published as *Travel Sketches* in 1988 are snapshotlike in their seemingly arbitrary cropping, suggesting moments rapidly recorded along a casual stroll—an effect he tries to replicate in his nonetheless tautly composed buildings.

Finally, for Tadao Ando the seventeenth-century Japanese "stroll garden," epitomized by the Katsura Detached Villa, became a model for the composition of projects such as the Koshino House completed in 1982. At first sight its plan appears anything but "Picturesque," but the journey through the interior is surprisingly complex. Animated by carefully calculated glimpses of the surrounding landscape and by the changing play of light across

the concrete walls, it was conceived, Ando says, as a sequence of individual scenes to be encountered sequentially along an architectural promenade. ∎

IDEA № 67

FIVE POINTS OF A NEW ARCHITECTURE

Le Corbusier's worldwide influence depended as much on his talent for presenting his work in words, drawings, and photographs as on the inventiveness and beauty of his buildings. He wrote more than 50 books and disseminated his buildings and projects through the eight volumes of *L'Œuvre Complète*, or "The Complete Architectural Works."

In the first of these—on pages 128–29—the reader discovers "LES 5 POINTS D'UNE ARCHITECTURE NOUVELLE," followed by the Maison Cook of 1926, in which they are seen at work.

Presented in words and diagrams that captured the essence of the new architecture by comparing it with the traditional forms it was intended to replace, the "Five Points" all derived from the possibilities offered by a new way of building using a reinforced concrete structural frame. In essence they had been anticipated more than 12 years earlier with the Dom-Ino House project that Le Corbusier proposed in 1914 as a response to the destruction of houses in the early months of the First World War. This had been intended as a factory-produced system of precast concrete columns, floor slabs, and staircase on which families could improvise shelter by recycling materials and components from destroyed houses.

Although the Dom-Ino House is often presented as an icon of the new architecture, Le Corbusier said it took him ten years to appreciate the full architectural implications of the structural frame, which he summed up as:

1. The *piloti*: hitherto constrained by the need to carry floor and roof loads, walls were liberated by a grid of columns or *piloti*.

2. The roof garden: the ground floor of the house could be lifted free of the ground; the basement—which he regarded as unhealthy and referred to elsewhere as "tubercular"—eliminated; and the land lost to building recaptured by a roof garden on the flat roof.

3. The **free plan**: freed of their load-bearing role, walls could now be arranged at will according to functional requirements and spatial ideas.

4. The ribbon window: as openings were no longer part of a load-bearing wall, ribbon windows could run horizontally across the facade. Le Corbusier claimed, misleadingly, that they would give a better quality of light, but their role was primarily formal: to present a striking contrast to traditional upright **windows**, and to represent the decentered, free spatial composition within.

5. The free facade: an elaboration of (4), emphasizing the new freedom to arrange openings according to functional and formal requirements.

Although associated with what later became known as the **International Style**, these ideas informed Le Corbusier's work throughout his career. In his town-planning projects the open ground floor became part of a continuous pedestrian realm; a 1933 project for Algiers proposed stacking suspended, serviced floors as "artificial ground" on which individual houses could be built; and in the series of Unités d'Habitation apartment blocks (see p.160) built in the 1950s, the roof garden became a shared space in which to relax and exercise under the sky. ∎

With its freestanding columns (or piloti), free facade of ribbon windows, open plan, and generous roof gardens, Le Corbusier's Villa Savoye (1928–30) is the definitive expression of his "Five Points of a New Architecture."

"The new architecture free of specific cultural associations."

In designing the Einstein Tower (1919–24)—a solar observatory—Erich Mendelsohn developed an expressive, abstract form to suggest the dynamism and conceptual ideas of modern physics.

A pure, formal language

ABOVE: *In his "Cardboard Houses" of the 1970s, Peter Eisenman sought a total abstraction based on the early language of Modern architecture— so total that he said he only assigned functions to spaces after finalizing the spatial composition.*

BELOW: *With its use of square grids to control the volumetric composition and constructional details, Frank Lloyd Wright's Unity Temple (1906) in Oak Park, Chicago, achieved a level of abstraction unequaled by then in Europe.*

IDEA № 68
ABSTRACTION

In the arts abstraction has come to mean work that does not depict a subject—more strictly "non-figurative" or "non-objective" art—and as such was one of the defining features of Modernism. In architecture abstraction has found its clearest expression in the International Style and recent examples such as Peter Eisenman's formalism.

The first manifesto advocating abstraction, *Concerning the Spiritual in Art*, was published in 1912 by the Russian painter Wassily Kandinsky, who was active in the German Expressionist circles from which the first fully abstract building, the Einstein Tower (opposite) by Erich Mendelsohn, emerged in 1914. It could be argued that the slightly earlier houses of the Viennese architect Adolf Loos (see p.134) deserve that accolade; however Loos reserved abstract neutrality for the exterior only, as a shield for the expressivity of the private interior.

By the early 1920s rigorous forms of abstraction were being practiced across Europe and the dominant trend toward abstraction in architecture, later christened the **International Style**, was characterized by clear geometric forms, white or plain-colored surfaces, and the extensive use of large sheets of **glass**. It was glass that made possible—in theory, if not always in experiential practice— the ultimate form of abstraction, transparency. Its proponents saw this new language as expressive of the Machine Age and universally applicable. This could be achieved, they believed, because the new architecture was seen as free of specific cultural associations and used a "pure" formal language that supposedly appealed directly to the human brain. The naivety of such views is now all too well known, but they must be understood historically, as an attempt to see the world in the light of redemption after the global conflagration of the First World War.

Abstraction was seen not only as a radically new form of expression but also as a means of "keeping inviolate"—to use the words of the English critic Herbert Read (he was writing in 1935)—the timeless qualities of art and architecture. This was why Frank Lloyd Wright could describe his advocacy of new ideas as a "Cause Conservative" and Le Corbusier could advocate architectural revolution while extoling the eternal "Lessons of Rome"—not for nothing was his first book on architecture published, in 1923, under the title *Vers une architecture* (Toward an architecture), with no hint of the "new" added to the title of the English translation four years later.

Abstraction has informed various attempts to understand architecture as an autonomous language, including Peter Eisenman's use of formal transformations that emulated the grammars described by the linguist Noam Chomsky, and John Hejduk's

research into the fundamental elements of architecture, which, through his teaching as head of New York's Cooper Union, influenced several generations of students. Although widely criticized by **Postmodernists**, abstraction continues to find favor among practitioners and clients. Indeed, stripped of its earlier ideological baggage it arguably became—often in the guise of various forms of minimalism—the dominant stylistic mode of the *fin de siècle*. ∎

The house of glass

IDEA № 69
TRANSPARENCY

Physical transparency made possible by large sheets of plate glass became one of the defining features of much Modern architecture, making possible—given suitable lighting conditions—both visual continuity of **space** between inside and out, and the revelation of the "truth" of the internal structure.

Mussolini's declaration that "Fascism is a house of glass" found compelling, if unintended, expression in Giuseppe Terragni's Casa del Fascio in Como (1936) in which the Classical containment of space and the spatial fluidity and transparency made possible by glass seem to coexist.

It was also deployed, in what Colin Rowe and Robert Slutzky have described as "phenomenal" transparency, as a means of indicating spatial depth through the **layering** of planes.

Transparency carried various other ideological meanings within the rhetoric of Modernity. Opening up hitherto closed spaces to light and air was seen as a means of promoting health—hence the early adoption of Modernist architecture for health centers and, especially, tuberculosis sanatoria, such as Alvar Aalto's Paimio Sanatorium (1928–33, pp.120–21).

Transparency was also seen as a means of promoting a social democratic society. In democratic societies physical transparency increasingly became an emblem of the (supposed) openness of government. This was given conspicuous expression, for example, in Norman Foster's reconstruction of the Reichstag in Berlin, where the masonry dome destroyed in the Second World War was recreated in glass and made publicly accessible to enable the inhabitants of the reunified Germany and Europe to partake visually in the process of democracy that can be glimpsed in the chamber below.

More broadly, transparency has been interpreted by the French critic Henri Lefebvre as an illusory device that has its origins in Greek thought, an approach to the world based on mathematical logic and reason.

Lefebvre interprets the transparency of Gothic architecture as a means of replacing the "dark" world of myth by the radiant light of God, bringing Christianity out of buried crypts and making it transparent to the eye.

The tectonic transparency and constructional "truth" of Gustave Eiffel's structures were adopted by the French state as emblems of its capacity to produce a rational world of science and technology, and Eiffel himself delighted in the "transparency" to calculation of iron structures compared to the difficulty of quantifying traditional masonry constructions. And nowhere has the symbolic opening up of knowledge received more monumental expression than in Paris, in Dominique Perrault's Bibliothèque Nationale, where book-stacks were opened to public gaze by encasing them in four transparent L-shaped towers. The towers overheated, however, and the stacks had to be moved underground—a fitting symbol, for some, of the frequently illusory character of transparency. ∎

Completed in 1994, Jean Nouvel's building for the Cartier Foundation for Contemporary Art epitomizes the spatial richness and ambiguity made possible by layering transparent planes of glass.

Drawing to scale in three dimensions

Many of the illustrations in Auguste Choisy's Histoire de l'Architecture (1899) used "worm's eye" axonometric views to show how a building's plan and form were interrelated.

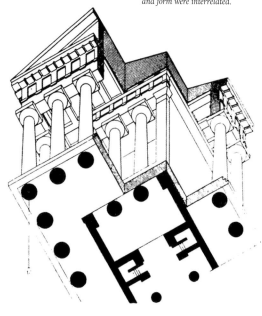

IDEA Nº 70
AXONOMETRIC PROJECTION

Axonometric projection is one of several means of representing a three-dimensional object on a two-dimensional surface; unlike the more familiar technique of **perspective projection** it does not suggest how the object might appear to the eye. Lines do not converge to one or more vanishing points but remain parallel, enabling all dimensions to be preserved true to the chosen scale.

Although axonometric projection did not become significant in architecture until the nineteenth century, its development occurred in parallel with perspective drawing. The earliest extensive use of axonometry was in calculating the trajectory of artillery projectiles, and it was widely taught to engineers rather than architects—and hence identified with industrialization and mechanization. In architecture, it extended the scientific basis for architectural representation offered by descriptive geometry and, not surprisingly, was favored at the French Ecole Polytechnique rather than at the Ecole des Beaux-arts.

The earliest widely influential uses of axonometric drawings also emanate from France. First were the graphical analyses made by the great theorist of constructional rationalism, Eugène Emmanuel Viollet-le-Duc (1814–79). Viollet-le-Duc's drawings emphasize an understanding of architecture as a three-dimensional system and it is thought that he derived the now familiar "exploded" axonometric technique from scientific texts on geology and anatomy. Like the great anatomist Georges Cuvier, whose ideas may well have influenced him, Viollet-le-Duc emphasized the role of each

"organ" in the larger system of the architectural "body."

Later, published in 1899, came the seminal illustrations by Auguste Choisy (1841–1909) in his book *Histoire de l'Architecture*. An engineer by training, Choisy integrated the orthographic projections of plan, section, and elevation into a single drawing, giving the illusion of a perspective drawing while remaining true to scale along all three axes. The drawings were highly effective in describing buildings as constructed "spatial organisms" and were reproduced by Le Corbusier in the 1920s and later emulated by Louis Kahn in presenting his own work.

Axonometric projections found favor among early Modernists for two contrasting reasons. To those committed to shaping an architecture for the Machine Age, they evoked the objectivity of science and technology, while to others of a more metaphysical inclination such as Theo van Doesburg, leader of the Dutch De Stijl movement, the rather different "objectivity" of gravity-defying colored planes floating in an infinite spatial field was effectively evoked without implying the presence of an observer (opposite).

Among more recent architects none, arguably, made greater or more

telling use of axonometry than Sir James Stirling. The "aerial view" of the Engineering Building at Leicester University (1959–63), designed with James Gowan, suggests that the entire building, with its 45-degree roof lights and chamfers, was designed in dialog with the chosen mode of projection. Later, in presenting a widely admired series of competition projects that culminated in the construction of the extension to the Staatsgalerie in Stuttgart (1977–83, pp.138–39), Stirling emulated Choisy's "worm's-eye" views projected upward from a plan to create beguiling drawings that both describe the three-dimensional **architectural promenade** through the building and evoke the episodic approach to **composition** that generated them. ∎

Theo van Doesburg, the founder of the Dutch De Stijl movement, employed abstract colored planes and axonometric projection to evoke his vision of an ideal spiritual world, floating free of gravity.

"Collage can enrich a work both formally and semantically."

Alvar Aalto's Villa Mairea (1937–40) is a thoroughgoing example of architectural collage: from the structural fragments seen on the entrance elevation to the vernacular-inspired pergolas, every detail and material conjured up associations familiar to its owners.

Patchwork of materials and forms

IDEA Nº 71
COLLAGE

The practice of piecing together materials to create a work of art has deep roots, but collage—from the French *coller*, to glue—is now used to refer to a compositional technique invented by Pablo Picasso and Georges Braque as a means of enriching their early Cubist works.

In using "real" materials—such as wine labels, bus or theater tickets, or scraps of wallpaper—the Cubists' aim was to enrich a work both formally and semantically. Materials were chosen to evoke specific associations or milieus in the viewer's mind, or newspapers clippings were selected for their content—Picasso repeatedly used reports of bomb outrages and other stories that suggested the unsettled political climate immediately before the First World War.

Although it was one of the most pervasive compositional techniques in Modernism, the use of collage in architecture was limited. The plans of Le Corbusier's houses of the 1920s can be seen as collagelike, and the Surrealist-inspired roof of his De Bestegui apartment, with its mobile hedges, outdoor fireplace, and its incorporation of the distant Arc de Triomphe as an "ornament," exploited the ability of collage to tie together disparate materials with strong associations.

Arguably the most potent architectural collage was produced away from the centers of early innovation, by Alvar Aalto in the Villa Mairea (1937–40, opposite). Built for the industrialists Harry and Maire Gullichsen near Noormarkku on Finland's west coast, the villa was intended to be a manifesto for Finland's place in the modern world, international in outlook yet rooted in the national culture and landscape. Aalto created a **free plan** that evoked traditional farmhouse interiors and populated it with rattan- and birch-strip-wrapped columns that echoed the gold banding of the pine trees in the surrounding forest, created by the shedding of their bark. Across the garden-courtyard the wooden sauna's flat roof was covered in turf, recalling traditional wooden buildings, and the sauna was tied back to the main house by a low stone wall modeled on medieval churchyards.

The Villa Mairea was exceptional in Aalto's work, and it was only with the advent of **Postmodernism** that overt collage-compositions became common. Michael Graves' early "Cubist kitchen" extensions emphasized the collagelike quality latent in the Corbusian syntax, and in their influential book *Collage City*, published in 1987, Colin Rowe and Fred Koetter argued for a view of the city that accepted multiple ordering systems and a palimpsest-like layering of time. Simultaneously in architecture designers such as Robert Venturi and Charles Moore pioneered the playful incorporation of Classical and other "borrowed" elements typical of the multivalent Postmodern style promoted by the critic Charles Jencks. In one of the major buildings of the 1980s, Stirling Wilford's extension to the Staatsgalerie in Stuttgart (pp.138–39), the composition echoes the Classical main building and is overlaid with references to other architectures, from the "High-tech" costume jewelry of its entrance canopies to Le Corbusier's double-house on the city's Weissenhof exhibition site. ■

Using planes to create architectural space

IDEA № 72

LAYERING

The term "layering" is widely, if often rather loosely, used to denote a compositional strategy that derives from Cubism. Rejecting perspective as a means of suggesting three-dimensional space, Cubists constructed their pictures from opaque, translucent, or apparently transparent planes.

In place of the deep illusory space that had been conventional in Western art since the Renaissance, their canvases suggested a pictorial space that was shallow and built up from multiple layers.

In two provocative essays entitled "Transparency: literal and phenomenal," published in 1963 and 1971, Colin Rowe and Robert Slutzky attempted to link architecture directly to Cubism by arguing that the early villas of Le Corbusier, and of the Villa Stein at Garches in particular, were conceived frontally and "pictorially" as a series of shallow layers—in some cases very shallow: they suggested, for example, that at Garches the window frames were conceived as a spatial layer passing behind the glass.

Although Colin Rowe later distanced himself from aspects of the "Transparency" articles, they were widely influential, encouraging architects to think of buildings as layered compositions—an approach that would be promoted by the advent of **computer-aided design** (CAD) software that requires buildings to be represented as multiple layers of data. Conceptually, the layers of a composition might be formal, material, or temporal.

Temporal layering was pioneered in Italy as an approach to **conservation** that became widely known through the work of Carlo Scarpa. In the Castelvecchio in Verona (1959–73, right top), for example, Scarpa implemented a series of demolitions, interventions, and additions that aimed to clarify the building's complex history. New work was rigorously distinguished from old by imposing an orthogonal geometry and by the choice of materials and detailing. New floors became independent layers, visibly "floating" within and over the old fabric, while the new glazing, framed in metal, was laid over the inside of the existing openings: seen from outside, it suggests a continuous new elevation that appears and disappears from view—much like the formal layers that Rowe and Slutzky saw in Le Corbusier's work. Scarpa's approach was indebted to a similar reading of Modernist space, in particular of some of the shallowest of all pictorial spaces encountered in the work of Piet Mondrian and the Dutch De Stijl movement.

As a formal strategy, layering finds its most provocative expression in **Deconstructionist** projects such as Bernard Tschumi's Parc de la Villette and in many designs by Peter Eisenman. In his 1983 proposal at Checkpoint Charlie in Berlin Eisenman "excavated" the site using historic maps to discover hidden layers that could be manipulated in the design of the new building. His Wexner Center for the Visual Arts at the University of Ohio in Columbus (see p.199), completed in 1989, was similarly designed by overlaying multiple layers of spatial order. Some were purely formal—the Modernist **grid**, represented by a steel "scaffolding"; others site-specific, such as the play on the offset of the campus grid from that of the city, which followed the Jefferson Grid; and others —notably the fragments of a demolished brick "fortress"—were narrative. ■

TOP: *At the Castelvecchio in Verona Carlo Scarpa articulated the different phases of the museum as a series of layers: here, rectilinear, bronze-framed glazing slides behind a Gothic arcaded opening.*

ABOVE: *The rough granite of Peter Celsing's Bank of Sweden, completed in 1976, recalls the rustication of Renaissance palazzi but the shifted, double-layered facade is quintessentially Modernist.*

Designed by Alison and Peter Smithson for one of Oxford University's women-only colleges, the Garden Building at St. Hilda's (1968–70) secures privacy behind a fully glazed facade by layering climbing plants, wooden pergola, and curtains.

"Conceptually, the layers of a composition might be formal, material, or temporal."

MAIN IMAGE: *Originally coined in 1930, the term "International Style" was even more appropriate to describe the global spread of the steel-and-glass style developed by Mies van der Rohe, seen here at its most luxuriant in the bronze-clad Seagram Building (1954–58) in New York.*

OPPOSITE: *Inspired by the success of the Stockholm International Exhibition of 1930, the International Style found a more enthusiastic welcome in Sweden than in much of Western Europe. The Södra Ängby villa district west of Stockholm fused Modernist architecture and Garden City planning to create an outstanding residential district.*

The style of the Machine Age

IDEA № 73

INTERNATIONAL STYLE

Henry-Russell Hitchcock and Philip Johnson identified three key features of the International Style in a book published to accompany the International Exhibition of Modern Architecture held at New York's Museum of Modern Art in 1932: the expression of volume rather than mass; dynamic balance rather than imposed symmetry; and the elimination of applied ornament.

These formal qualities had emerged in various developments of the 1920s in Europe: the Dutch De Stijl movement; the work of Le Corbusier, whose **Five Points of a New Architecture** were the first attempt to codify the new vision; and in Germany, in the work of Mies van der Rohe and the Bauhaus circle centered around Walter Gropius. Although a universally applicable architecture, expressive of the **Zeitgeist** of the emerging Machine Age, was a shared ideal common to many of these architects and movements, the idea that this architecture was simply the latest "style" among the many

identified by art historians was certainly not. By emphasizing its most readily identifiable formal qualities, Hitchcock and Johnson ignored or underplayed the radical social ideals that were inseparable from much of the European work—principles such as "truth to materials," which underpinned its aesthetic expression, and the spatial innovations of the **free plan** that were, arguably, its most potent contribution to architectural thought.

The Weissenhof Estate, built as part of a major housing exhibition in Stuttgart in 1927 and featuring the

work of 15 leading European Modernist architects, is widely recognized as a key manifestation of the emerging International Style. It was, by then, being widely adopted in Eastern Europe and proved equally congenial as an expression of the rather different social democratic ideals of Scandinavia, where it was known as Functionalism or "Funkis" and, frequently merged with English Garden City ideals, formed the basis for both social and middle-class housing—the villa district of Södra Ängby (left) in western Stockholm built in 1933–40 being an outstanding example.

The exodus of Modern architects from Nazi Germany was a key factor in the spread of the International Style. It led to the world's greatest concentration of such buildings in Israel and, with Walter Gropius installed at Harvard University and Mies van der Rohe in what became the Illinois Institute of Technology in Chicago, set the scene for the U.S. to develop and promote what became a truly global style after the Second World War. The dominant formal language was derived from Mies's steel-and-glass style—which crystallized in the Farnsworth House (see p.154), apartments at 860–880 Lake Shore Drive in Chicago, and in the Seagram Building (opposite) in New York—while a key vehicle for its dissemination was the emergence of large corporate practices such as Skidmore Owings and Merrill, or SOM as they were later rebranded, which were scaled and organized to serve global corporations. ∎

Distilling the essence of a design

IDEA № 74

LESS IS MORE

One of the very few aphorisms coined by an architect to enter the popular language, "less is more" was used by Mies van der Rohe to express his approach to two aspects of his work: to base the architectural expression on the essential elements of a structure and to eliminate visual clutter.

The first referred to the "skin and bones" of the building, as he called them, such as the cladding and steel frame. The second was a process of aesthetic reduction that aimed to eliminate visual clutter by suppressing secondary elements of a building and thereby heighten the visual impact of a space or view, the material qualities of surfaces, and the play of light across them.

The latter approach reflects the influence of seventeenth-century Sukiya-style Japanese architecture, exemplified by the Katsura Detached Villa, and was seen at its most poetic in Mies's Barcelona Pavilion (pp.124–25). It can also be related to the formal means of the Dutch De Stijl movement, although their aspirations—to express through the use of lines and colored planes the underlying structure of the universe—were rather more ambitious.

"Less is more" would hardly have achieved the currency it enjoys had it not captured an aesthetic ideal that became pervasive in twentieth-century architecture, often misleadingly referred to by the term "Minimalism"—misleadingly because of the confusion it invites with the narrower intentions of the eponymous 1960s art movement. The term Minimalist can reasonably be applied to an otherwise diverse range of contemporary practitioners, from Eduardo Souto de Moura to Peter Zumthor, Alberto Campo Baeza to Yoshio Taniguchi, Alvaro Siza to Tadao Ando, as well as to those who overtly espouse it, such as John Pawson—whose 1996 book *Minimal* enjoyed considerable popular success.

In architecture, particularly at the domestic scale, Minimalist design can be seen as a reaction against all kinds of clutter—from radiators and electrical sockets on walls, to the overabundance of consumer goods—and, in a broader historical perspective, as a response to the disappearance of craftsmanship. In place of ornament, as the Viennese architects Otto Wagner and Adolf Loos realized toward the end of the nineteenth century, the architect would increasingly come to rely on the "luxury" of fine surfaces—in the Barcelona Pavilion the sense of luxury was palpable, courtesy of expensive natural materials. In the work of the Mexican Luis Barragán it comes courtesy of intense color and light, and in the buildings of Tadao Ando from the play of sunlight across concrete walls of exquisite refinement.

Despite its suppression of all expressions of overt craftsmanship, Minimalist design places considerable demands on both designer and builder. Traditionally, building was a process of successive approximation, moving from roughly worked to finely finished materials and using a repertoire of devices—skirtings, casings, etc.—to cover junctions between surfaces and components. By eliminating these to emphasise the "purity" of the planes that compose a space, less-is-more design heightens our awareness of the beauty of materials and surfaces, but also of any lapses from precision in their making. ∎

Less-is-more design heightens our awareness of the beauty of materials and surfaces.

All-white, inside and out, the resolutely plain surfaces of Alberto Campo Baeza's Gaspar House in Cádiz, Spain epitomizes the growing interest in Minimalist expression in the late twentieth century.

As a movement Regionalism came into vogue in the wake of the Second World War, but no building exemplifies its ideals more fully than Frank Lloyd Wright's desert home and studio, Taliesin West, which was substantially complete in 1937.

Responding to locality

IDEA № 75
REGIONALISM

Committed to a universal architecture for the Machine Age, the first generation of Modern architects deliberately ignored the local conditions of site and materials, and climate and culture, which traditionally influenced architectural design. Away from its centers of origin, however, the **International Style** was soon adapted to national or regional traditions.

BELOW: *With its large porch for outdoor living and redwood cladding, William Wurster's house for Robert and Deborah Green on Mt. Diablo, California (1938) was later seen as a pioneering example of the Bay Region Style promoted by Lewis Mumford in an influential article published in 1947.*

BOTTOM: *The interior of Alvar Aalto's Villa Mairea in Noormarkku, Finland (1937–40) was conceived as an abstraction of the coniferous forests that still occupy most of the country's land.*

Rejecting a "rootless modern architecture," for example, Alvar Aalto's Villa Mairea (right bottom) was overlaid, **collage**-like, with allusions to vernacular and Modern architecture, while inside rattan- and birch-strip-wrapped columns evoked the Finnish forest.

Following the Second World War an avowedly Regionalist school that had been developing in the Bay Region of California came to international attention courtesy of the wood-clad domestic buildings of architects such as William Wurster (right top) and Pietro Belluschi. More overtly Modern in their extensive use of steel and glass, but similarly regional in epitomizing the Californian lifestyle, were the Case Study houses promoted by John Entenza—most famous among them that built by Charles and Ray Eames in 1949.

Promoting the Bay Region work in the *New Yorker* in 1947, Lewis Mumford argued that Regionalism and Modernism need not be opposed—indeed, by allowing regional variations Modern architecture could become truly international and move beyond "its adolescent period, with its quixotic purities, its awkward self-consciousness, its assertive dogmatism." His ideas were vigorously rejected by New York's Modernist establishment, but thanks to the exhibition "America Builds," shown in Sweden during the war and in Denmark immediately after

it, young Scandinavian architects were encouraged to cross the Atlantic to see the new Regionalist work, as well as that of Frank Lloyd Wright, whose responsiveness to site was legendary. Their experiences influenced the "softened" Modernism that developed in Scandinavia, and while this clearly reflected the region's social democratic ideals, timber resources, and vernacular traditions, it quickly came to influence architecture and lifestyles worldwide, eventually becoming—courtesy of IKEA—the most widely diffused style in history.

Attempting to come to terms with the ethical dilemmas of practicing in a globalized world, Alexander Tzonis and Liane Lefaivre coined the term "Critical Regionalism" in an essay entitled "The Grid and the Pathway," published in 1981. They argued that while welcoming the benefits of interaction and exchange, designers should think critically about their impact and value the uniqueness of the local/regional culture, environment, and resources. In this way they hoped to avoid both the commercialization of "folk" traditions and their political use—as in Hitler's promotion of *volkisch* culture—as a means of excluding others.

This approach was quickly taken up and disseminated by Kenneth Frampton through several versions of an article originally entitled "Towards a Critical Regionalism: Six Points for an Architecture of Resistance." Drawing

on **phenomenology**, Frampton argued for an emphasis on topography, climate, light, and the tactile rather than the visual. Advocating **tectonic** rather than **scenographic** form as exemplary of such an approach, he advocated the work of Aalto, Jørn Utzon, and, later, Tadao Ando, among others. Ando's houses, described by the architect as "bastions of resistance" against the Western consumerism that was swamping traditional Japanese culture, epitomized the "critical" ideal. ∎

Transformable buildings

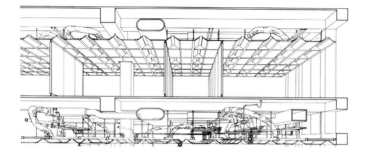

IDEA № 76
FLEXIBILITY

A concern for greater flexibility in buildings arose in the 1950s as a reaction against the excesses of **form follows function**, which argued that all parts of a building should be determined by, and destined for, specific uses. In practice, however, even if these uses could be determined, no allowance was made for new developments over time, let alone the changes of use that happen in many buildings.

Designing for flexibility also addressed a contradiction identified by Walter Gropius: that although the architect's ultimate concern was expected to be the use and occupation of buildings, his involvement generally ceased at the moment occupation began.

Early Modernist architecture offered two celebrated examples of built-in flexibility: Gerrit Rietveld's Schröder House of 1924 in Utrecht (see p.137), in which the second floor could be transformed each evening from an open living space into private bedrooms in a manner that recalls the adaptability of the traditional Japanese house; and Pierre Chareau's Maison de Verre in Paris, which featured a series of pivoting and sliding screens and storage units, a stair that could be lifted and lowered, and other devices to accommodate its combined use as home and doctor's surgery.

In the 1950s in the U.S. Ezra Ehrenkrantz and Konrad Wachsmann took a more radical approach by developing building systems in which all the services were confined to the ceiling space and the interior was subdivided by demountable partitions (above). In Europe these ideas were extended by Cedric Price, Yona Friedman, and Constant Nieuwenhuys into Utopian visions of flexible cities made of transformable, even mobile, buildings.

TOP LEFT: *Ezra Ehrenkrantz's Construction System with its lightweight frame construction and ceiling packed with services, was an early and widely influential model of designed-in flexibility.*

ABOVE: *With its clear span of 246ft (75m) Renzo Piano's and Richard Rogers' Pompidou Center in Paris was a structural tour de force intended to provide totally flexible, highly serviced open spaces. Walls for hanging pictures and framing spaces were added later to create a more conventional gallery arrangement.*

More practical than these technical fixes was the development of the open plan. Most buildings prior to the mid-seventeenth century were predicated on a similar sort of flexibility, as the functional differentiation made possible by the invention of the **corridor** had not yet arrived. Palladio's villas, for example, were entirely unspecific as to the use of their different rooms; in some villas even the lavatories were used as thoroughfares in the interconnected matrix of rooms. The impact of the open plan was widely felt in the transformation of office work that began in the 1940s in the U.S., and was extended in the 1950s and 1960s by Eberhard & Wolfgang Schnelle in Germany through the development of Bürolandschaft: freed from partitions, large well-lit and serviced spaces acquired an open, landscapelike feeling that was often enhanced by the strategic placing of large pot plants.

The best-known critique of such approaches to flexibility came in the Netherlands, where Aldo van Eyck and Herman Hertzberger emphasized the importance of how the user interprets a given form or space, and advocated the use of archetypal forms that were open to many interpretations or uses. Hertzberger also proposed that buildings should be left incomplete or unfinished, so as to invite the occupants to appropriate them. At his Centraal Beheer Offices, for example, the employees completed the deliberately gray and bare concrete and block structure by bringing in their own decorations, plants, and memorabilia of their domestic lives. ■

Beauty of raw concrete

IDEA № 77
BETON BRUT

Viewing concrete as an artificial, industrial product, Le Corbusier at first attempted to use it in a way that suggested the smoothness and precision of machines. Later he came to appreciate the rough texture of the "brute" board-marked surfaces. *Béton brut* (French for rough concrete) and Brutalism were born.

Nowhere was the gulf between the rhetoric about a Machine Age architecture and the realities of building more apparent than in the use of reinforced concrete. For a workers' housing development the Cité Frugès in Pessac (1923–24), Le Corbusier experimented with pumping concrete into reusable formwork, but the results were so crude and the color so dull that the walls had to be painted. In the 1920s villas the radiant white "concrete" is frequently a composite of reinforced concrete frame and traditional blockwork and plaster.

After the Second World War, faced with building the Unité d'Habitation in Marseilles (above), Le Corbusier initially envisaged—if his own account is to be believed—an exposed but relatively even finish. The builders, assuming that the concrete was to be plastered, took little care to achieve this, and, faced with what he described as "a massacre of concrete," Le Corbusier decided to embrace the rough, board-marked surfaces—"Let us keep all that brute," he declared. *Béton brut* was born and with it, unwittingly, the name of a movement: reported in the British press, the master's new material was embraced by the young architects Alison and Peter Smithson to describe an emerging attitude. Brutalism gained currency following the publication of Reyner Banham's 1966 book, *The New Brutalism. Ethic or Aesthetic?*, but it was an uneasy alliance of two tendencies: an international interest in rough materials, and an expression of the Utopian socialist values espoused by the Smithsons.

The brute quality of the Unité was equally apparent in the Jaoul Houses, in which Le Corbusier contrasted raw concrete and rough brickwork with finely detailed hardwood. The bricks came "by the heap load" from demolition sites and their use was ethical as well as aesthetic: "We are not bourgeois," Le Corbusier declared, "we appreciate the beauty of the raw brick." Appropriately enough, it was a religious order that gave him the opportunity to create his greatest essay in *béton brut*, the monastery of La Tourette, north of Lyon. It is instructive to compare the visual character of its surfaces with those of the later Carpenter Center at Harvard. The latter is, by "normal" standards, far better built, but visually its neatly shuttered concrete lacks the visual vitality of that at the monastery. Not so much board-marked as board-splattered, La Tourette manages to combine raw power with a delicate inner radiance.

Having learned to see concrete as a natural material "of the same rank as stone, wood, or baked earth," Le Corbusier increasingly came to relish the juxtaposition of different textures, colors, and materials in his buildings, anticipating the recent preoccupation with materiality in architecture. His choice was not just aesthetic, but emblematic of his interest in vernacular cultures, and the loss of faith in technological progress that led him to project a vision at once archaic and modern. ∎

ABOVE LEFT: *Faced with a tight budget in building his Unité d'Habitation in Marseilles, Le Corbusier decided to make a virtue of the concrete straight from its rough-wood formwork, christening it "béton brut."*

In England, the Corbusian béton brut *aesthetic spawned what later became known as Brutalism—a term frequently seen as negative by the general public when confronted by buildings like Chamberlin Powell and Bon's controversial Barbican Centre (shown here) in central London.*

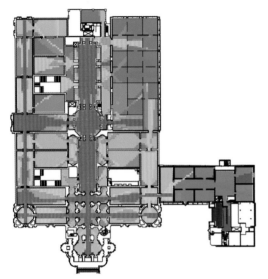

Although most widely used in urban design, the technique of Space Syntax is now yielding interesting results in analyzing and predicting visitor movement in buildings, as seen here in Kali Tzortzi's studies of the Tate Britain (below) and Tate Modern (below right) galleries in London.

IDEA № 78

MORPHOLOGY

Architectural morphology describes the underlying logic of form in architecture. Also known as "configurational studies," it emphasizes the fundamental geometric determinants of, and limits to, the organization of space.

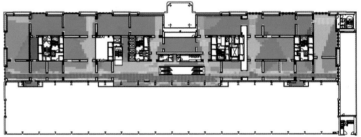

Conceived independently by the polymath Goethe and German physiologist Karl Friedrich Burdach (1776–1847), morphology originally described the study of the form, formation, and transformation of living organisms. To those inclined to think of buildings biologically, as **organisms**, its relevance to architecture is obvious.

Much of the contemporary research into architectural morphology grew out of the pioneering Centre for Land Use and Built Form Studies at Cambridge University, England, where Leslie Martin and his colleagues initially addressed the simple-seeming question: "What building forms make the best use of land?" Their most influential finding concluded that, assuming common standards of daylighting were applied, low-rise perimeter or courtyard developments could achieve similar, or even higher, densities when compared with the then still widely favored model of high-rise towers in open space.

The architects' department at the London Borough of Merton quickly confirmed the validity of the theoretical argument with large housing developments at Pollards Hill (1971) and Eastfields (1974). The former consisted of a series of three-story P-shaped blocks, with alternating culs-de-sac and amenity spaces, and achieved a density of 116 persons per acre, higher than the London County Council's celebrated Roehampton Estates where the buildings rose to 11 stories.

Similar approaches have more recently been applied to studies of the energy efficiency of different urban forms, but the impact on practice of a growing body of academic research worldwide—much of it promoted through the journal *Environment and Planning B*—has been relatively modest. A notable exception, however, is the field called Space Syntax. This became widely known through *The Social Logic of Space* (1984) by Bill Hillier and Julienne Hanson, and its analytical techniques to evaluate the role of spatial layout in shaping patterns of human behavior are now applied internationally in developing layouts for urban designs, retail environments, and other large-scale proposals.

An altogether more personal use of morphology was made by the Finnish architect Reima Pietilä (1923–93). In a 1958 essay entitled "The Morphology of Expressive Space" he lamented the fact that architecture could still be understood by means of Euclidean geometry, whereas nature—"the apotheosis of plasticity"—was far more complex and elusive in form. In the exhibition *Morphology and Urbanism* held in Helsinki in 1960, Pietilä illustrated his approach with abstract formal analyses of different types of city planning and elegant, Lego-like "Stick Studies" that anticipated aspects of the Systems Art of the 1960s. Natural metaphors loomed increasingly large in his mature work in such overtly "geological" projects as the Dipoli Students' Center in Otaniemi (1961–66) and Mica Moraine; the latter was the motto for his competition-winning Official Residence of the President of the Finnish Republic (1983–93) and celebrated the last glaciation of the Finnish landscape. ■

undertook an imaginative series of morphological studies of natural phenomena: supremely elegant, the resulting drawings and models exerted a decisive influence on his later architectural work.

Growing room by room

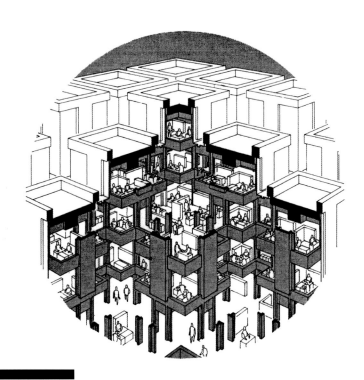

IDEA Nº 79
ADDITIVE COMPOSITION

The plans of most buildings are created by a process of adding rooms—or groups of rooms—together, or by subdividing an overall shape. Purely additive compositions are found frequently in vernacular buildings—Italian *trulli*, for example, grow room by room, each dwelling clearly identified by its distinctive conical roof—but were latecomers to formal architecture.

They found favor as a means of achieving Picturesque effects, as in the more rambling plans of Norman Shaw or American "Shingle Style" houses; of responding to the varied functions accommodated by a complex building—Alvar Aalto's Paimio Sanatorium (1928–33, see pp.120–21) is an assemblage of discrete functional elements; or of expressing the elements of a composition, such as the servant and served spaces of Louis Kahn's Richards Medical Laboratories (1957–61, see p.166)

In the mid-twentieth century, however, what might be termed the "additive principle" assumed particular significance in a body of work that has become known as Dutch structuralism, and in a series of projects by Jørn Utzon. Utzon took inspiration from the architect Wim van Bodegraven's 1952 call for structures that could develop over time while retaining their coherence and meaning, and from Aldo van Eyck's celebrated Amsterdam orphanage (1957–60). Planned as an assemblage of individual "houses" using a legible "kit of parts," the orphanage recalls vernacular settlements van Eyck had studied in Africa.

Piet Blom and Joop van Stigt's 1962 project for a "Village of Children" offered a beguiling image of flexibility and order based on the repetition of a precast structure, ideas given powerful expression by Herman Hertzberger in his Centraal Beheer offices in Apeldoorn (1967–72, above and opposite). Although generated by the repetition of a single spatial/structural unit, the interior offered—to use a phrase of van Eyck's—a "labyrinthian clarity." In thoroughgoing additive compositions, giving emphasis to the main entrance often presents a problem, but here its suppression was an expression of the management policy, which allowed employees to come and go unsupervised.

In Jørn Utzon's work the term "additive" was chosen to suggest a relationship to the cellular growth of natural forms. The power of the additive principle dawned on him while at play, arranging leaves and flowers, and pointing out to his son the seemingly endless variety nature could generate from a modest number of elements. Fused with memories of the cellular structures of Islamic cities it informed a succession of projects that began in 1966 with an overtly bazaar-like competition project for Farum town center, Denmark, and concluded with an unrealized project for a sports complex in Jeddah, Saudi Arabia, which marshaled a small palette of precast concrete components to evoke a compelling image of the complexity of nature. After falling out of favor, such a compositional approach is being given new life by **parametric design** software. ∎

building could echo
"growing" by
gained wider
950s and 1960s.
rger's Centraal
n Apeldoorn (main
diagram opposite)
compelling built
dea: its entire form
the repetition
patial unit.

"Today we must build with hollow stones."

Louis Kahn's insistence on separating and expressing a building's "servant" and "served" space is seen here at its most dramatic in his Richards Medical Laboratories in Philadelphia.

Separation of services and usable space

With its external glass elevators and prefabricated stainless steel WC "pods," Richard Rogers's Lloyds Building in London echoes Louis Kahn's articulation of "servant" spaces.

IDEA № 80
SERVANT AND SERVED SPACES

Organizing a building into "servant and served spaces" was the idea of the American architect Louis Kahn. He realized that the growing demand for mechanical services of all kinds in modern buildings—from air-conditioning ducts to elevators—could be met by housing them in apparently solid, masonrylike enclosures or "servant" spaces, and that this idea could be extended by distinguishing all a building's spaces into "servant and served."

The idea came to Kahn (1901–74) during a spell as resident architect at the American School in Rome in the early 1950s, during which time he traveled around the Mediterranean and encountered, as if for the first time, the power of masonry architecture for which his education under the French Beaux-Arts system at the University of Pennsylvania had been an ideal preparation.

Kahn was by then too orthodox a Modernist to suggest—as exponents of **Postmodernism** would later do—that it was admissible to build with "fake" thick walls and heavy columns and he later proclaimed: "Today we must build with hollow stones." This idea seems to have occurred to Kahn as a result of visiting Scottish castles, where he saw how minor spaces, staircases, and so on had been hollowed out of the massive defensive walls.

The first building in which the idea of servant and served spaces was realized was a modest but potent affair—a bathhouse (changing rooms)

for an outdoor swimming pool at the Jewish Community Center in Trenton, New Jersey (1954). This consisted of four pyramidal roofs surmounting square rooms "served" by "hollow columns" that acted as baffled entrances or contained WCs. With the completion of the Richards Medical Laboratories at the University of Pennsylvania (opposite) in 1961, "servant and served spaces" were given potent expression as brick towers containing elevators, escape stairs, and service ducts grouped around square laboratory towers. The building brought Kahn to world attention and was frequently compared to the profile of the Italian hill town of San Gimignano, with its cluster of slender towers, though Kahn vigorously denied any such **Picturesque** intention.

Although accepted as Kahn's idea, the principle of organizing complex buildings in a manner that echoed the principle of "servant and served" became increasingly common. It could be said to underpin Sydney Opera

House (1957–73, see p.39), for example, where Jørn Utzon—similarly inspired by ancient structures, in his case Mayan temples—divided the accommodation between the public spaces of auditoria, restaurant, and foyers housed in the celebrated shells, and all non-public functions in the stepped platform below. And it was also much favored by British exponents of High-tech such as Norman Foster and Richard Rogers. The former's Sainsbury Centre at East Anglia University (1974–78) consists of a "service zone" wrapped around a Miesian universal space (see **free plan**), while Rogers's Lloyd's Building (1979–86, above) in London is, with its external stairs, elevators, and WC "pods," Kahnian in organization if not expression. ∎

Ambiguous architecture of metaphor and allusion

IDEA № 81

POSTMODERNISM

The term "Postmodernism" came into common usage in the 1980s to describe a broad range of tendencies in culture and politics. Postmodernists question any central hierarchy or organizing principle, preferring ambiguity, diversity, and interconnectedness.

Postmodernism was greatly influenced by the disillusionment that followed the Second World War, and its proponents, who distrusted all universalizing theories and ideologies, drew attention—often through the critical method known as **Deconstruction**—to the conventions and assumptions that underpin different practices.

In architecture, Postmodernism was in part a response to the growing formalism of the **International Style** in the 1950s and its emergence was marked by two key books: *Complexity and Contradiction in Architecture* by Robert Venturi (1966) and *The Language of Post-Modern Architecture* by the historian and critic Charles Jencks (1978). As his title suggests, Jencks viewed architecture primarily as a means of communication, and brought to its interpretation a range of ideas from literary criticism, such as metaphor, syntax, and symbolism. Against the Modernist emphasis on clarity of space and structure he favored elements that were "double-coded" and ambiguous. And in place of stylistic originality and purity, he argued for the eclectic use of elements from past styles.

Jencks did not see Postmodernism as rejecting Modernism *tout court*, but as using its innovations selectively—architects like Michael Graves (in his early work) and Peter Eisenman, for example, drew heavily on such spatial ideas as **collage** and **layering** developed by Le Corbusier in particular in the 1920s. Like Venturi, Jencks praised **regional** expressions of identity and the **everyday** world of the American strip mall and suburban housing, and advocated the "knowing" incorporation of vernacular elements in forms drawn from "high" traditions such as Classicism.

By pinning his colors to the mast of what many architects saw as deeply flawed **scenographic** projects—such as Michael Graves's Portland Public Services Building (1980, opposite) and Charles Moore's Piazza d'Italia in New Orleans (1976–79)—Jencks did little to commend his cause to those committed to **tectonic** expression as the basis of architectural form, but his ideas proved widely influential. His book went into several editions and was followed by a succession of special issues of the magazine *Architectural Design*, in which Jencks presented supposedly "new" styles, from "Free-Style Classicism" to "Abstract Representation," "Post-Modern Classicism" to "Late-Modern Architecture." Twenty-five years on from the heyday of architectural Postmodernism it seems clear that its advocacy of overt stylistic eclecticism yielded few buildings of lasting merit; the late work of James Stirling—such as the extension to the Staatsgalerie in Stuttgart (see pp.138–39)—is a notable exception. Postmodern thought continues, however, to inform assumptions that underpin most current practice, and its lasting legacy may well prove to be in the pervasive interest in the "specificity" of architectural design in responding to site, materials, and program. ∎

Arata Isozaki's Tsukuba Science Center in Japan epitomizes the stylistic eclecticism of Postmodernism, its design freely mingling forms drawn from Western Modernism and Classicism with others from native Japanese traditions.

"Nonstraightforward architecture"

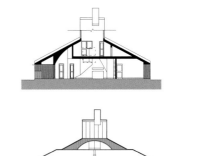

IDEA № 82

COMPLEXITY AND CONTRADICTION

This idea—or bundle of ideas—is taken from the title of a 1966 book that the historian and critic Vincent Scully described in his preface as "probably the most important writing on the making of architecture since Le Corbusier's *Vers une architecture.*" The full title was *Complexity and Contradiction in Architecture,* and it was written by the American architect Robert Venturi, who offered it as "a gentle manifesto" for "a nonstraightforward architecture."

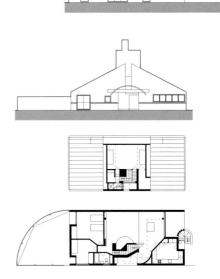

Its influence has been pervasive and many memorable phrases Venturi used to sum up his ideas have entered the language of the design studio: "both-and"; "the difficult whole"; "Main Street is almost all right"; "contradiction juxtaposed."

Historically, Venturi's book can be seen as the first major salvo in what would later be recognized as architectural **Postmodernism**. Rejecting the **form follows function** dogma and judgemental attitudes that he thought pervaded Modern architecture, Venturi invited architects to look at both architectural history and the everyday world ("Main Street"). Declaring that "less is a bore" he advocated ambiguity and distortion over the "purity" of the **International Style** and, while fascinated by pop culture, he also had a voracious appetite for the history of architecture, with a notable penchant for its more arcane phases, such as Italian Mannerism. He looked to both as sources of compositional ideas and

"effects" with scant regard for any deeper historical understanding of why they had been deployed in a given work.

Although offering a frontal assault on Modern architecture as practiced in the 1960s, Venturi by no means rejected it completely. His favorite targets were what one might call "the great simplifiers"—most obviously Mies van der Rohe, but also Frank Lloyd Wright. He disliked, for example, Wright's obsessive suppression of diagonals in projects such as Fallingwater (see p.61), whereas he praised Alvar Aalto's use of double skins in shaping indoor space, or the contrast between the crowded complexity of the plans of Le Corbusier's Villa Savoye (see p.141) and its simple-seeming elevations.

Significant in the success of Venturi's book was the fact that it concluded with a selection of his own projects in which the ideas were put to work. These included the house (above and opposite) he designed for his mother, Vanna Venturi, in 1962,

which was destined to become an icon of Postmodernism. It greets the visitor with a conspicuously houselike gable, but this almost childlike image is undermined by the Mannerist device of a split gable. Similarly, a familiar, small-paned square window is juxtaposed (contradictorily...) to a Corbusian ribbon window. In plan, the entrance, chimney, and stair compete for centrality and are distorted in the process, while spatially the house combines both rooms and a Modern volumetric space.

As a demonstration of an architectural approach, the "Mother's House" as it became known could hardly have been clearer. But nor could the weaknesses of an approach that viewed architecture as a repertoire of compositional devices divorced from any concern with the logic of building; and that sought to produce meaning through a repertoire of signs, not embody it through a hard-won and genuinely difficult whole. ∎

"Main Street is almost all right."

In Robert Venturi's "Mother's House" (1961–64) in Philadelphia familiar domestic forms are rendered "complex" by celebrating rather than suppressing "contradictory" compositional demands.

Cheap buildings with decorated fronts

IDEA Nº 83

SHED

Opening his celebrated book *An Outline of European Architecture* (1942), Nikolaus Pevsner made a now infamous distinction between architecture and building: "a bicycle shed is a building; Lincoln Cathedral is a piece of architecture... the term architecture applies only to buildings designed with a view to aesthetic appeal."

As a definition this begged the question not only as to the nature and sources of "aesthetic appeal," but also as to why a bicycle shed could not possess it: the aesthetic merits of larger, shedlike industrial buildings had, after all, been greatly admired by the pioneers of Modern design whose cause Pevsner espoused.

As a basic form of enclosure, the shed exerted a wide appeal in the twentieth century, but the currency of the term owes much to an analysis of the Las Vegas strip, published in 1972 as *Learning from Las Vegas* by Robert Venturi, Denise Scott Brown, and Steve Izenour. The authors suggest that all buildings may be described as either "ducks" or "decorated sheds." The model for the former was a Long Island restaurant built in the shape of a duck, declaring through its form the food it offered. The typical Las Vegas casino, by contrast, was a vast, deep-plan "shed"

with a lavish illuminated sign to announce its attractions to people in passing cars.

The authors went on to suggest that all buildings could be considered in this way: modern, "functionalist" ones attempting to convey purpose through expensive and often, in their view, needlessly contrived form, whereas many traditional ones—they used Amiens Cathedral (see p.26) and the Doge's Palace (opposite top) as examples—were organized as cheap sheds with declamatory, decorated fronts: their aim was rhetorical, but the reductive nature of such a view is spectacular. Its relevance for many contemporary building programs, however, was obvious, resonating with **Postmodernism's** emerging discourse about meaning in architecture: the "decorated shed" quickly entered the language of architecture.

More recently, in a provocative assault on architectural pretensions entitled *Terminal Architecture* (1998), the English critic Martin Pawley eulogizes the vast sheds erected by industry and commerce, from major production plants to the storage and distribution facilities that cluster around highway intersections. In Europe, the latter began to appear in the 1970s and during the 1980s, Pawley claims, "a million out-of-town commercial and retail centres sprang up to join them." His point is twofold: this vast transformation took place with almost no "architectural" input and, he argues, it offers a better model than the outdated values by which most architects operate.

Comparing a Cadbury's Easter egg store and distribution center near Birmingham with the fraught, 35-year saga of building the British Library, in

London Pawley suggests that the former does much the same job as the library at a fraction of the cost, and would have offered a better alternative to a monumental "temple" housing an outmoded form of knowledge storage. However uncongenial to most architects Pawley's views may be, like its ancient relative, the **primitive hut**, the shed, decorated or otherwise, is surely destined to exert a continuing fascination as a "degree zero" of architecture. ■

ABOVE: *With its elaborate stone front and plain brick sides the Doge's Palace in Venice is typical of the traditional buildings that Robert Venturi reductively categorized as "decorated sheds."*

RIGHT: *Groups of large warehouses and factories clustered around major highway junctions became a feature of industrial development in the 1980s: this example is outside the city of Newport in south Wales.*

This 1978 vision of the city by Aldo Rossi (1931–97), which he titled *"Great Urban Construction"* (Grande costruzione urbana), *evokes an almost dreamlike world inhabited by what he saw as persisting, fundamental architectural forms or types.*

The memory of space

TYPE

In Giulio Carlo Argan's 1962 essay "On the Typology of Architecture" a type is defined as an historically derived "formal" consensus, which, despite all the variations throughout history, will always look essentially the same, although the use may change dramatically.

ABOVE: *At the heart of the Italian town of Lucca is an oval group of buildings occupying the remains of a Roman amphitheater—an example of what Aldo Rossi called the "memory" of the city.*

BELOW: *Rossi's Modena Cemetery (1972–) was conceived as a "city of the dead" that conflates memories of tomb, house, and urban forms.*

Like its close Platonic relatives **form** and idea, "type" has acquired specific associations in architecture. These stem from the the *Historical Dictionary of Architecture* published by the French archaeologist and historian Quatremère de Quincy in 1825:

> The orderly art of building was born from a pre-existing seed. Everything must have an antecedent; nothing whatsoever comes from nothing, and this cannot but apply to all human inventions. We observe also how all inventions, in spite of subsequent changes, have conserved their elementary principle in a manner that is always visible... This is what ought to be called type in architecture as in every other area of human invention and institution.

This conservative conception was uncongenial to the Modernist belief in originality, and it was only in 1962 that Quatremère's ideas resurfaced in mainstream thought, courtesy of Giulio Carlo Argan's essay. The type, in Argan's conception, is not an ideal from which one may not deviate, but the source of historical meanings that change only gradually. And as the repository of historic types, the fabric of the city must be treated with respect, and should not be subject to wholesale redevelopment.

In the English-speaking world the idea of type was also explored in a widely discussed 1967 essay by Alan Colquhoun entitled "Typology and Design Method." Challenging the claim of Functionalists that an architectural form could be arrived at purely empirically from the demands of the program and site, Colquhoun stressed that these could constrain but never determine form, and that in designing, the architect necessarily made formal decisions that drew on preexisting types. In tune with the structuralist ideas that were widely influential at the time, Colquhoun stressed that these formal decisions were essentially arbitrary and conventional, rooted in the culture of architecture, not in some supposed quasi-scientific objectivity.

Argan's ideas were a major influence on the Italian Neo-Rationalists Carlo Aymonino, Giorgio Grassi, and Aldo Rossi (1931–97), as seen in the latter's book *The Architecture of the City* (1966). Rossi's ideas eventually crystallized around the idea of "analogical architecture." He saw architecture as the "memory" of the city, and argued that buildings—like human memories—may be either "pathological" or "propelling." Key memories, embodied in "urban artifacts," must be permanent but also allow, and even act as catalysts for, change. The building type, therefore,

preserves its general form but is open to new uses, and just as human memory, working by analogy, is often vague, allusive, and dreamlike, so architects ought to aim at evoking similar qualities in their work. In the design of his celebrated cemetery at Modena (above), for example, Rossi evokes memories of tomb, house, city, and cemetery, conflating them into a new, previously nonexistent synthesis in which each is seen to contain the others, thereby embodying a poignant meditation on life and death. ■

IDEA № 85
CONTEXT

The belief that an architectural design should "respond" or "relate" to its context is recent, and has diverse roots: the development of conservation movements; architects' rediscovery of the city as a repository of cultural "memory" and building "types"; the development of urban design as an independent discipline; the search for regional identity; and the **Postmodern** rejection of objective truths and universal cultural narratives.

In architecture, the Postmodern belief that all knowledge and experience are produced in specific cultural and physical contexts was mediated by the growing interest in **phenomenology**, with its contention that people, things, and buildings can only be understood when seen as fully integrated in the world.

Architects' attempts to give expression to the idea of a building as "enmeshed" in its context predate such Postmodern concerns. Frank Lloyd Wright famously observed that a building should be "of" not "on" a hill, and his life's work demonstrated a succession of attempts to integrate building and site: the horizontal lines of

"A building should be 'of,' not 'on,' a hill."

his Prairie Style houses, the geologically stratified form of Fallingwater (see p.61), the incomparable "desert architecture" of Taliesin West (see p.156) that responds to both the landscape and Native American culture—all attest to his ability to work with the unique qualities of different localities. Wrightian in spirit, too, is a recent, widely acclaimed "contextual" project, the exquisite swimming pools by which Alvaro Siza articulates the meeting of land and sea near Porto in Portugal (above right).

In the wake of Postmodernism, the response to context—especially in urban settings—has stimulated diverse approaches. The widely emulated "dancing mullions" of Rafael Moneo's town hall in Murcia, for example, were originally conceived as an abstraction of the formal rhythms underlying the Baroque cathedral at the other end of the square. In the Neue Staatsgalerie extension in Stuttgart (see pp.138–39), by contrast, Stirling and Wilford offer more direct and disparate "references"

to the context: the massing responds to the contrasting frontages of the street and highway that frame the site; the plan echoes the Neoclassical main building and the generic Classical type with a domed main room—which here appears "in ruins" as an open rotunda; the music wing has a grand-piano-shaped plan that generates acoustically appropriate rooms but also recalls a favored Modernist motif; and the library is designed as an echo of the massing and fenestration of Le Corbusier's double-villa across the city on the Weissenhof exhibition site.

A similarly vigorous engagement with an urban context can be seen in Enric Miralles' extension to Utrecht Town Hall (above left). The existing complex was a labyrinthine and impenetrable amalgam of some ten medieval buildings and city castles that Miralles was asked to transform into an open, transparent, and inviting complex. His approach was radical, layering old and new into an architectural **collage** that preserves the

best of the old while destabilizing its familiarity. For both Miralles and Stirling and Wilford the "context" is a complex amalgam of locality and architectural history, something in which all buildings are now seen as inescapably bound up. ■

ABOVE: Two "four-poster" aedicules
that rise to ridge roof lights frame
particular "places" within the
otherwise open plan of Charles
Moore's house in Orinda,
California (1962).

RIGHT: Although recognized as a
classic example of the Modernist free
plan, the vast living floor of Mies van
der Rohe's Tugendhat House in Brno
(1930) anticipates later ideas about
"place"—as seen here, for example,
in the semicircular Macassar
ebony screen that frames the black
pearwood dining table.

The building as a space for an occasion

The central spine of Aldo van Eyck's orphanage building in Amsterdam was conceived as an indoor "street" offering opportunities for the children to meet, sit, and play.

IDEA № 86
PLACE

The now ubiquitous word "place" was introduced into architecture in the 1950s by the Dutch architect Aldo van Eyck and became the focus of an influential postwar critique of the **International Style**.

His use of the term is best known through a characteristically poetic 1962 text entitled "Place and Occasion," which is worth quoting at length:

Space has no room, time not a moment for us. / We are excluded. / In order to be included—to help our homecoming—we must be gathered into their meaning / ... Whatever space and time mean, place and occasion mean more. / For space in our image is place, and time in our image is occasion. /... so start with this: articulate the in-between. Make / a welcome of each door / a countenance of each window. Make of each a place; a bunch of places of each house and each city / (a house is a tiny city, a city a huge house).

In the spirit of concreteness that van Eyck espoused, the architectural implications of his ideas are best seen in the building that became a manifesto for them, the Amsterdam Orphanage (1957–60, above). Conceived as a "tiny city" organized around a streetlike circulation spine, the orphanage was an **additive composition** of centralized units—square and shallow-domed—rendered diverse and richly habitable by changes of level and light, child-scaled built-in furnishings, free-standing lamps and a host of other details. Doors were made "places for an occasion" by swelling the ground slab into semicircular steps, and even the walls and floors recognize the children's presence courtesy of tiny embedded mirrors.

Van Eyck's ideas were highly influential, nowhere more so than on America's West Coast, where Charles Moore built for himself a vacation house in Orinda, California (opposite, top), that epitomizes on a tiny scale the place-making approach to architecture. The square **free plan** is articulated by what Moore called two "four-posters": open, aedicular structures reminiscent of Laugier's **primitive hut**, they have pyramidal "roofs" that rise to a roof light along the ridge, creating a **particular** light that reinforces the feeling of "place" made for the bed and the open, sunken bath. Moore's ideas and work were widely disseminated through the book *The Place of Houses*: written with Gerald Allen and Donlyn Lyndon and first published in 1974, it remains in print.

The emphasis on place was readily extended to urban and landscape design, where it related to the ancient idea of **genius loci**, and although it undoubtedly signaled a shift toward what would later become known as **Postmodern** thought, it would be misleading to suggest that its qualities were absent from earlier Modern architecture. The bathroom of Le Corbusier's Villa Savoye, with its roof light and tiled chaise longue, is every bit as much a **particular** place for bathing as Moore's in Orinda, and there can be few more luxurious "places" in which to dine than Mies van der Rohe's Tugendhat House (opposite bottom), where the monumental dining table is framed by a semicircular partition lined with richly figured, book-matched veneers of exotic Macassar wood. ∎

The bodily experience of the building

IDEA № 87

PHENOMENOLOGY

Phenomenology is a strand of continental European philosophy that aims to understand the world from the experience of being an embodied presence in it. Applied to architecture, a phenomenological perspective endeavors to ensure that the primacy of experience is not lost in addressing the complexities or sheer size of modern developments, or sacrificed to the allure of abstract systems of spatial **composition** that fail to recognize the difference between lived **place** and geometric **space**.

With its textured surfaces and rich play of colored light, Steven Holl's Chapel of St. Ignatius in Seattle offers worshipers an intensely sensual vision of spiritual experience.

Although Hegel used the word phenomenology in the eighteenth century, contemporary understanding of the concept in philosophy—and in architecture—comes primarily from Edmund Husserl, Martin Heidegger, and Maurice Merleau-Ponty. The idea has been widely taken up in architecture, beginning in the 1970s through the writings of influential historians and critics such as Christian Norberg-Schulz, Dalibor Vesely, and Kenneth Frampton.

A significant factor in the diffusion of thought in architecture inspired by phenomenology was the 1958 book *The Poetics of Space* by the French philosopher Gaston Bachelard, which became something of a "cult" text in architecture schools in the 1970s and 1980s. Basing his analysis of the foundations of architecture on our lived experience of buildings—not, as had been attempted in Enlightenment thought, on its purported origins (see **primitive hut**)—Bachelard analyzed poetry to reveal the qualities of such fundamental (domestic) spatial types as the attic, the cellar, and drawers. In doing so, he implicitly encouraged architects to base their work on the experiences it will engender rather than on abstract ideas.

A key idea in phenomenology is the "lifeworld," which refers to the taken-for-granted context of daily life to which normally people pay no conscious attention. Through a change in perspective—the **phenomenological reduction** as it is sometimes called—phenomenological analysis aims to bring to the **everyday** a reflective, sympathetic attitude.

An influential generation of architectural phenomenologists, including David Leatherbarrow and Alberto Pérez-Goméz, emerged under the teaching of Dalibor Vesely and Joseph Rykwert at the University of Essex in England in the 1970s, while more recently the writings of the Finnish architect and theorist Juhani Pallasmaa, such as *The Eyes of the Skin* (1996), have been popular in schools of architecture. The widespread diffusion of phenomenological ideas is apparent in the growing interest in designing for the senses by emphasizing the play of shadow and light, pursuing the tactile use of materials, and seeking an almost theatrical choreography of atmosphere. Among today's leading practitioners both Steven Holl and Peter Zumthor have declared themselves "architectural phenomenologists," while in Japan Tadao Ando draws on traditional ideas

about bodily experience to place a similar emphasis on the quality of light and tactility of surfaces. For many, Zumthor's brooding, atmospheric Thermal Baths at Vals (1996, opposite), with their richly textured stone walls and dramatic fissures of light slashed through the concrete roof slab, epitomize the phenomenological emphasis on the experiential basis of architecture. But it is equally apparent in Holl's love of washes of colored light, tactile materials, and snaking ramps and stairs calculated to heighten the experience of bodily movement through space. ∎

Designed to engage all our senses, Peter Zumthor's Thermal Baths at Vals in Switzerland epitomize the design implications of the thoroughgoing concern with bodily experience encouraged by engagement with phenomenological ideas.

The building's outer layer

ABOVE: *The slick surfaces and then provocative use of color mark Eero Saarinen's General Motors Technical Center, Michigan, as a forerunner of the recent fascination with the skin of buildings.*

BELOW: *Modeled on foam, the ETFE cushions of the Water Cube swimming complex, built for the Beijing Olympics, offered a striking new approach to shaping the building envelope.*

IDEA № 88

SKIN

The word "skin' is now in common usage to describe the outer layer(s) of a building. Its adoption reflects two recent trends: the tendency promoted by innovations such as **rainscreen cladding** to view the exterior as largely autonomous from the interior; and a growing awareness that the building envelope needs to be a complex environmental filter that plays a key role in **passive design**.

The first trend is epitomized by the voluptuous surfaces of Frank Gehry's buildings, such as the Bilbao Guggenheim Museum (see p.198) or the Disney Concert Hall in Los Angeles, and by the so-called Swiss Box school represented by architects such as Herzog and de Meuron, Peter Zumthor, and Gigon Guyer. Gehry's forms are partly inspired by the flowing, folded fabrics depicted in eighteenth-century portraits, while in an interview in 1993 Herzog and de Meuron said their aim was to push any material they use "to an extreme to show it dismantled from any other function than 'being.'" Gigon Guyer talk of "the alchemy of materials" and specialize in the unexpected: placing glass directly over insulation as the skin of a solid wall on the Kirchner Museum in Davos (1989–92), for example, challenges our assumptions about the "nature" of glass.

Viewed biologically, the skin of a building can be seen as both stretched over the spatial "organs" within—an image evoked by many **computer-aided-design**-generated projects (and rather fewer actual buildings to date)—and as a means of regulating the interaction of interior and exterior. The latter approach is associated primarily with multilayered glass facades in which different types of glass and coatings can be tuned to give the desired environmental performance.

The most literal expression of the building envelope as a skin is made possible by architectural fabrics, and although fabric structures go back to the beginnings of architecture—Sir Banister Fletcher illustrates a tent on the first plate of his celebrated "Comparative History" of architecture—their development for large, permanent buildings has only been made possible by recent developments such as glass fiber coated with PTFE (polytetra-fluorethylene, best known by its DuPont brand name, Teflon), and the more recent ETFE (Ethylene etrafluoro-ethylene). The former is seen, for

example, on the Schlumberger research facility built in 1985 near Cambridge, England, by Michael Hopkins, where the fabric roof sweeps down to meet, albeit somewhat awkwardly, the rectilinear geometry of the steel and glass structure, while the celebrated Eden Centre in Cornwall, England, and Water Cube swimming center built for the 2008 Beijing Olympics are clad with inflated ETFE cushions.

With the advent of nanofibers and so-called intelligent fabrics, designers of future building skins will have at their disposal membrane structures made with woven photovoltaic skins and active shading systems. Similar developments in glass technologies look set to enable building skins of the future to come increasingly close to reflecting the complexity of real skin in mediating the interaction of internal and external environments. ∎

"The skin of a building can be seen as stretched over the spatial 'organs' within."

Conceived as a continuous plane that warped in response to the movement of visitors, Foreign Office Architects' Yokohama Terminal in Japan (1995–2002) was rationalized into a series of complex folded structures that exploited computer-aided design and manufacturing techniques to the full.

Drawing board of the digital architect

IDEA № 89

COMPUTER-AIDED DESIGN

Computer-generated visualizations—often of the "photo-real" kind—have become by far the commonest means of presenting designs to clients, planning committees, and the media. And a new generation of so-called digital architects are exploiting the potential of **parametric** form-generating software to design buildings that could not even have been conceived without CAD systems.

Like many forms of advanced technology, the roots of computer-aided design (CAD) began with the military. In the 1950s, the U.S. Air Force, working in association with the Massachusetts Institute of Technology (MIT), developed a system that combined cathode-ray tube displays and light-gun technology to target aircraft through radar and assign defense tactics. In 1960, Itek—a defense contractor manufacturing optical equipment in the U.S.—received funding to develop an interactive graphic system which became known as the Electronic Drafting Machine (EDM). Shortly after, back at MIT, a doctoral thesis by Ivan Sutherland called Sketchpad produced a prototype drafting system for engineering that led to the formation of a company called Applicon in 1968. Renamed Analytics, Inc., they developed commercial CAD machines, color inkjet plotters (the first appeared in 1977), and, after buying the license from another company in 1981, three-dimensional modeling software. The following year the company Autodesk was formed from a loose collaboration between programmers: it was destined to produce the most widely used CAD package for two-dimensional applications.

The costs of early CAD systems, and the hardware to run them on, limited their use in architecture, but with the advent of personal computers in the 1980s they were set to replace drawing boards in most offices. The advantages were obvious: they enabled easier coordination of the thousands of documents needed to build large projects, and could be readily updated—gone were the days of multiple scratched-out drawings held together with magic tape! And while some still lament the loss of hand-drawing skills, CAD has almost completely taken over the "production" or "working" drawings phase of architectural design—although the gestation of designs still generally involves hand-sketching and model-making.

The latest Building Information Modeling (BIM) systems have destroyed the old separation of two-dimensional drafting and three-dimensional modeling, bills of quantities, and other data sources in building, by using three-dimensional, real-time models that integrate geometry, spatial relationships, geographic information, and the quantities and properties of building components. Similarly, design and manufacturing systems (known as CADCAM) are eroding the division between designing and making. So-called 3D printers enable designs to be rapidly modeled, and CAD drawings or models may be sent directly to numerically controlled machines to produce an endless array of unique components, eliminating the traditional discipline of "rationalizing" a design into repetitive elements. Buildings like the Bilbao Guggenheim Museum (see p.198) exploit this potential to the full, although Frank Gehry's way of designing is unusual. Using software originally written to digitize wind-tunnel-tested models of fighter aircraft, he works like a sculptor, shaping his complex, billowing forms through physical models which are then scanned with a laser to produce a "point cloud" of data that enables them to be developed digitally. ∎

Protective skin laid over the building's structure

IDEA № 90
RAINSCREEN CLADDING

Rainscreen cladding is a recent technical innovation with far-reaching practical and aesthetic implications. It involves hanging a thin panel of material—initially stone, now a wide variety of metals, woods, glass, and synthetic materials—from a backing wall using proprietary systems of metal rails and clips that create a cavity, typically 1–1¼in (25–30mm) deep, to allow the movement of air.

The joints between the panels are also kept open and the ventilated cavity allows any water that penetrates to be removed, partly by evaporation and partly by running down the rear face of the panels and out at the bottom.

Originally developed as a response to problems with stone cladding, the system's advantages are various. It allows the use of thin, and therefore cheaper, panels (although there is growing concern that they may not last for the expected 60-year life); by enabling each panel to be fixed back to the structure, the stresses induced in traditional stone cladding systems are eliminated; by leaving joints open, the sealants whose failure is a major problem with older cladding systems are no longer required; finally, allowing the insulation to be placed on the outside of the backing wall eliminates cold bridges and allows the wall's mass to be used as a "thermal flywheel" to reduce energy consumption in the building, often as part of a broader **passive design** strategy.

Architecturally, however, the implications of rainscreen cladding are more problematic. They were wryly anticipated in Rem Koolhaas's observation, in his 1978 book *Delirious New York*, that "Technology + cardboard (or any other flimsy material) = REALITY." Koolhaas was referring to the cardboard illusions of the ephemeral "architecture" of Coney Island, but it is not a vast leap to the housing development near The Hague designed by his former members of staff, MVRDV, where more or less identical houses are arrayed in wood, terracotta, aluminum, and other materials. What rainscreen cladding enforces, more than any earlier form of construction, is a radical divorce between the inner structure of the building and its external appearance, rendering problematic many of the ideas—most obviously "truth to materials"—that have preoccupied architects and theorists since the advent of industrialization.

The expressive freedom allowed by rainscreen cladding has been widely exploited in recent architecture, creating an unexpected new market for suitable woods, such as the now globally ubiquitous western red cedar from North America, and for the more widespread use of thin sheets of "luxurious" materials like stainless steel and titanium—the latter being the preferred medium for Frank Gehry's exercises in billowing surfaces at the Bilbao Guggenheim Museum and elsewhere. In the hands of talented designers the results can be impressive, but in the world of commercial architecture the reduction of buildings to a durable but characterless structural "shell and core" with more or less ephemeral external "dressing" and internal "fit-out" seems problematic in a world increasingly preoccupied with meeting the challenges of **sustainable design. ■**

ABOVE: *In this hotel extension in Zurich, Burkhalter and Sumi use a wooden rainscreen to shield walls and conceal windows and balconies, allowing the building to be transformed by patterns of use.*

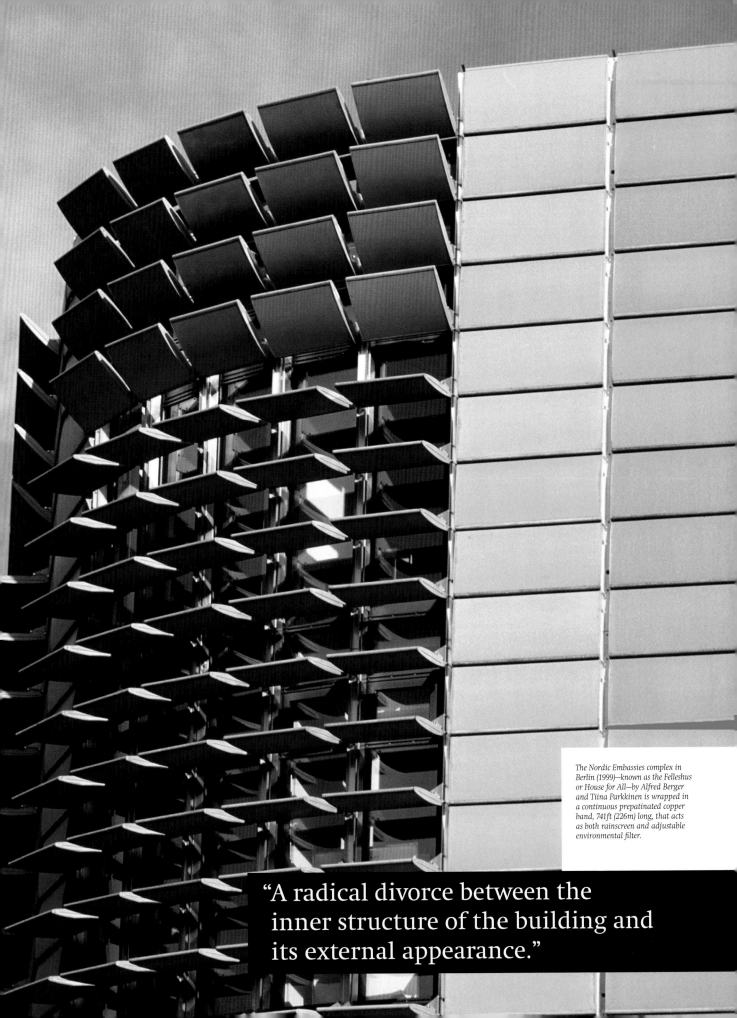

The Nordic Embassies complex in Berlin (1999)—known as the Felleshus or House for All—by Alfred Berger and Tiina Parkkinen is wrapped in a continuous prepatinated copper band, 741ft (226m) long, that acts as both rainscreen and adjustable environmental filter.

"A radical divorce between the inner structure of the building and its external appearance."

Architecture by everyone

Community architecture frequently fuses with self-build, encouraging clients to become part of the entire design and building process: above, constructing a Walter Segal House; below, erecting a wooden frame.

IDEA № 91

COMMUNITY ARCHITECTURE

The term "community architecture" was coined by the journalist Charles Knevitt in 1975 to describe an English housing movement that involved the participation of users in the design of buildings. It later came to embrace disparate trends that grew out of the political activism of the 1960s and growing concern about the impact of large-scale urban renewal—of which Jane Jacobs' book *The Death and Life of Great American Cities* offered a searing critique.

In England, a prime mover of community architecture was future RIBA president Rod Hackney who, while a graduate student at Manchester University, bought a house in Black Road, Macclesfield, only to discover that it was scheduled for demolition. Working with other families he instigated a regeneration scheme, with much of the work being self-built. Hackney had a flair for publicity and this was the catalyst for numerous community-based projects.

A major pioneer of self-build was the Swiss émigré Walter Segal, who designed his own wood-framed house in London's Highgate in the 1960s. It became the prototype for the Segal System for self-build and in the 1970s the London Borough of Lewisham made land available for a group of pioneers. Following Segal's death in 1985 a trust was formed to promote his system.

Although widely prized for their social value, few community architecture projects produced work of significant architectural merit. There were, however, notable exceptions. Ralph Erskine's widely admired Byker housing development in Newcastle upon Tyne (1969–80) was built after close consultation with residents, while in Belgium, Lucien Kroll's Medical Faculty Housing at the Université Catholique, Woluwe-Saint-Lambert, Brussels (1970–82) exhibited a controlled anarchy that was purportedly derived from the involvement of students in its design.

The most concerted attempt to theorize a participatory design process was made by Christopher Alexander, an English architect-academic who taught for many years at the University of California in Berkeley. His 1977 book *A Pattern Language* was based on an exhaustive analysis of traditional buildings and purported to offer a process to replace conventional methods and rediscover what he believed to be the universal values of "The Timeless Way of Building" (the title of a 1978 book).

The most interesting recent example of community architecture has been the work of the Rural Studio at Auburn University in Alabama. Founded by the inspirational architect and teacher Samuel Mockbee (1944–2001), Rural Studio is both an educational vehicle and a means of improving living conditions in one of the poorest regions in the U.S. It made a mark in 1994 with its first project, the Hay Bale House, built for a couple in their seventies who had been raising three grandchildren in a dilapidated shack. Deploying a radically contemporary aesthetic grounded in an appreciation of Southern vernacular forms, Mockbee and his students went on to produce a stream of inventive projects, most of which featured imaginatively salvaged or recycled materials. ■

*Beginning in the late 1960s
Walter Segal (1907–85) developed a
wood-framed building system that
eliminated the "wet" building trades
such as bricklaying and plastering to
enable relatively unskilled people to
build their own houses.*

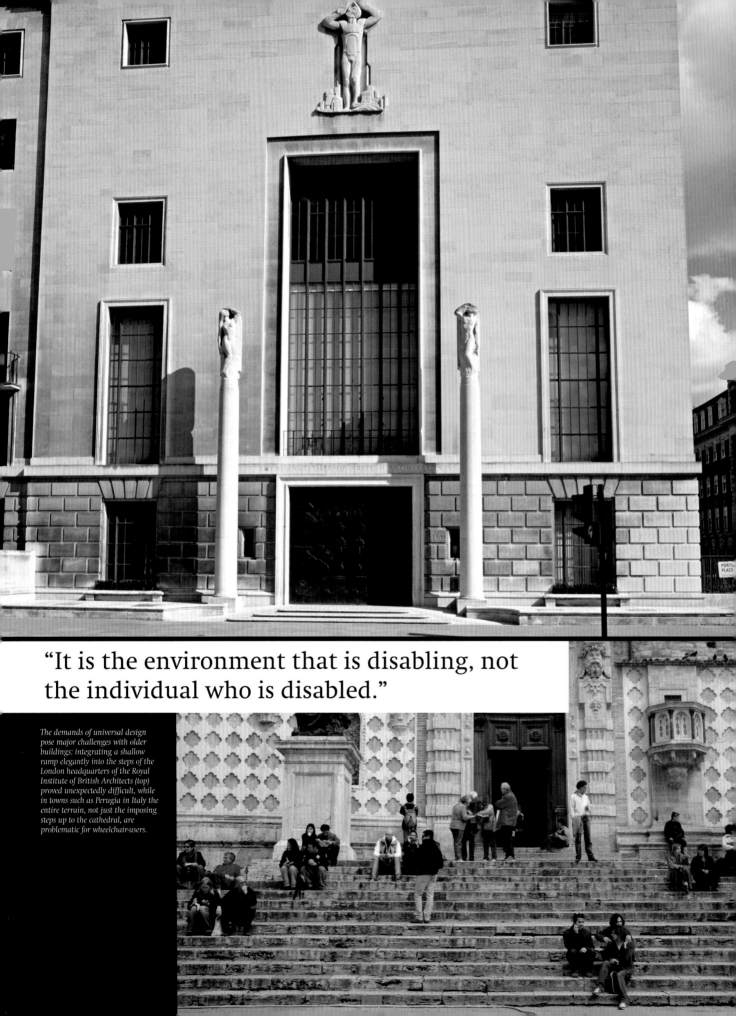

"It is the environment that is disabling, not the individual who is disabled."

The demands of universal design pose major challenges with older buildings: integrating a shallow ramp elegantly into the steps of the London headquarters of the Royal Institute of British Architects (top) proved unexpectedly difficult, while in towns such as Perugia in Italy the entire terrain, not just the imposing steps up to the cathedral, are problematic for wheelchair-users.

Designing accessibly for all

This bathroom by the U.S. company Kohler was designed to demonstrate that "normal" fittings could be used to meet universal design standards.

IDEA № 92
UNIVERSAL DESIGN

Designing to meet the needs of disabled people became a growing concern during the second half of the twentieth century, and by the 1990s had begun to be focused internationally around the idea of universal design.

This also embraced the concerns of the ageing "baby boomer" generation, and was influenced by the social model of disability that emerged in the U.K. in the 1980s, but had its roots in earlier and wider movements for civil and human rights. Its advocates propose that barriers, negative attitudes, and exclusion by society, intentionally or inadvertently, define who is disabled and who is not. In this view it is the environment that is disabling, not the individual who is disabled, and while it is recognized that individual differences may lead to individual limitations, these are not seen as the primary causes of social exclusion.

This increasingly accepted paradigm goes well beyond the traditional concern with physical accessibility. By promoting the design of buildings, products, and environments that are usable and effective for everyone, universal design recognizes the importance of how things look as well as how they perform.

As life expectancy rises and survival rates from major injuries, illnesses, and birth defects improve, interest in universal design goes well beyond the former, widely caricatured view of "disabled design" as being concerned primarily with people in wheelchairs. Disability is now seen not as a static characteristic of an individual but rather as an aspect of the dynamic relationship between the individual and the environment. Through more thoughtful design, everyone can be made more "able." If the general environment is more accommodating, people with disabilities may move about more easily and their need for assistive technology can then be correspondingly reduced.

Architecturally, the demands of universal design are far-reaching, but they address mostly matters of detail. It calls for ramps in place of, or alongside, short flights of steps; smooth ground surfaces at entrances to buildings, without stairs or steps; slightly wider interior doors to facilitate wheelchair access; the provision of accessible WC cubicles within male and female bathrooms, not separate from them; lever handles rather than twisting knobs; light switches with large flat panels rather than small toggle switches; bright lighting, particularly where visually demanding tasks are to be performed; clear lines of sight to reduce dependence on sound for those with hearing impairments; and so on.

The broader impact of addressing these issues seems likely to be in reducing the use of changes in level and illumination to differentiate parts of a building, the former because ramps suitable for wheelchair-users are often too space-consuming, the latter because of the needs of the visually impaired. Critics argue that excessive zeal in promoting such approaches could lead to an homogenization of buildings worldwide, not dissimilar to that of the late development of the **International Style**, which eventually produced the reaction in favor of the greater expression of **regional** and local identities that came with the rise of **Postmodernism.** ■

Fusing architect and builder

DESIGN AND BUILD

The separation of design from building was essential to the development of the **architect** as an independent professional, responsible for a building's design and for securing competitive bids for its construction. In many countries this division of responsibilities has been extended to a separation between "design" and "constructional design."

In the U.S., for example, most architects hand over the "detailing" to the contractor, while in France the separation between *architectes* and *bureaux d'études*, who ensure compliance with regulations and produce construction drawings, has deep roots in the **Beaux-Arts** view of architecture as an "art."

The size and complexity of many modern building programs necessitates numerous specialist consulting and subcontracting firms. Co-ordinating the flow of information between all the parties has become a major challenge, and the consequent potential for delays, and therefore increased costs, has greatly increased. "Design and build" is a response to this situation, and in the U.K. was specifically advocated in the Egan Report, "Rethinking Construction," published in 1998.

Arguing for greater integration of design and construction along the traditional "master builder" model, Sir John Egan's aim was a more seamless and "lean" process to increase efficiency. The major impact of his ideas, however, has been that architects

are increasingly employed by the contractor rather than the client. Alternatively, on prestigious projects or difficult sites, a "design" architect may be engaged to secure planning permission, and perhaps to produce "indicative details" for construction. The design may then be taken over by a design-build contractor who employs another (or sometimes the same) architect to develop the production drawings. The end price for the client is, in theory, fixed at this stage and increased costs are the responsibility of the contractor, which frequently results in a coarsening of details—curves become faceted, the quality of finishes is diminished.

The promised benefits of design and build—reduced financial risks for owners, shorter delivery time, greater communication between parties involved, a single source of accountability—has proved attractive in areas where cost and time overruns are critical.

For those concerned with the architectural quality, design–build is frequently problematic. The design process is routinely shortened,

sometimes severely curtailed, and as an employee of the contractor the architect has less authority over design decisions. Combining consultancy and contracting also reduces or diffuses accountability for the quality of the work. At the end of the project, for example, the process of "snagging" minor faults in workmanship, formerly undertaken by the architect independently to ensure compliance with the drawings and specification, places considerable reliance on the integrity of the design/construction team. For many clients, however, these disadvantages are outweighed by the perceived benefits and design–build appears destined to become the dominant form of building procurement. ∎

Vulcan House in Sheffield, England (the new home of the government's Border Agency, shown here) was procured using a design and build contract and designed to exceed the U.K. government's demanding environmental targets, leading to several sustainability awards. The design team was led by engineers Mott MacDonald.

Toward zero-energy architecture

PASSIVE DESIGN

Passive design describes an approach to achieving the required environmental conditions with the least possible use of "active," energy-consuming systems.

Prototypes for many contemporary passive design strategies can be found in traditional architecture, such as the four-directional wind-catchers seen here in the Iranian town of Yazd.

In particular, it aims to reduce dependence on artificial lighting, mechanical ventilation, and **air conditioning**. Although computer software is now used to model a building's performance, based on a sophisticated mathematical understanding of climate, heat transfer, and fluid dynamics, the fundamental principles have been practiced in vernacular buildings throughout history.

The single most important factor in traditional passive design was a building's orientation to the sun. Both the ancient Greeks and Chinese favored a southerly orientation whenever possible. In China, systems of geomancy that linked practical solar design to cosmological ideas about the sun, warmth, and health—best known today as Feng Shui—have survived in an unbroken tradition.

In the Middle East, where cooling was the main challenge, remarkably sophisticated ways of ventilating and cooling were developed. For example, wind-catchers (above) were used to draw air over porous earthenware pots full of water, which evaporated and cooled the surrounding air—a technique recently revived as passive downdraft evaporative cooling (PDEC), eye-catchingly used in conical fabric structures intended to cool open-air spaces at the Seville Expo of 1992. Ice houses in the Iranian desert consisting of a thick-walled storage chamber and tall walls shading a shallow pool of water, could even create ice passively, thanks to the cool night temperatures and thermal radiation to the black sky.

The first modern European passive solar houses were built in Germany following the First World War, while at the Bauhaus the Functionalist Hannes Meyer, who succeeded Walter Gropius as director, proposed the "maximal use of the sun (as) the best plan for construction" in order to achieve the health-giving properties of solar exposure. A concern for health was a major driver for passive design, seen at its most urgent in the tuberculosis sanatoria that rose across Europe (see pp.120–21).

In the U.S., George Keck pioneered the design of solar houses in the 1930s and 1940s, while Frank Lloyd Wright's earth-sheltered second Jacobs House of 1944, planned on a circular arc, was built in homage to the solar cycle. In Britain, the Building Research Station developed a now familiar device—the heliodon—for simulating the movement of the sun using an artificial lamp: it was enthusiastically reported in the *RIBA Journal* in 1931.

A key strategy of many "passive buildings" is to store daytime heat gains in their structure, and for this purpose a trombe wall system is sometimes used. Named after the

"The fundamental principles of passive design have been practiced in vernacular buildings throughout history."

The Solarsiedlung in Schlierberg near Freiburg by Rolf Disch Architects combines both passive (south-facing glazed facades shaded by adjustable awnings) and active (photovoltaic-cell-covered roofs) energy-design strategies.

French engineer Félix Trombe who developed it in the mid-1950s, it consists of insulated glass, a ventilated air cavity, and a thick wall to absorb the solar heat gains. Passive design gained momentum courtesy of the 1973 oil crisis, stimulating, particularly in the U.S., the publication of numerous books on solar design. Passive design principles are now widely practiced as part of the larger concern for sustainable design. ∎

Environmental architecture

IDEA № 95
SUSTAINABILITY

Making new buildings more energy efficient has led to the growth of **passive design**, but the early focus on running costs is now giving way to a more holistic concern for "cradle to grave" assessments that address a building's entire lifecycle or "ecological footprint."

Completed in 2002, the Beddington Zero Energy Development (now known universally as BedZED) is one of the most widely visited low-energy, sustainable housing developments in the U.K. Situated in Hackbridge, south London, it was designed by Bill Dunster Architects.

Global concern about the capacity of the planet to sustain a rapidly rising population without drastic environmental degradation came into sharp focus in 1987 with the publication of "Our Common Future," the report of the World Commission on Environment and Development (now generally referred to as the Brundtland Commission).

Its suggestion that "sustainable development" was the key to ongoing prosperity launched the idea of "sustainability" into the global consciousness. Such concerns were not new, however, and can be traced back to early responses to the Industrial Revolution and the start of the mass consumption of fossil fuels.

The consumption of natural resources grew exponentially in the last century, and with this came a growing scientific awareness of the interdependence of life, which led to the emergence of ecology as a separate discipline. The publication in 1962 of Rachel Carson's book *Silent Spring*, which documented the rapid growth in destructive technologies, from pesticides such as DDT to synthetic materials and nuclear power, has been widely seen as a catalyst for environmental movements that led to today's Greenpeace and Friends of the Earth. In 1972, the Club of Rome, an influential international non-governmental organization now headquartered in Switzerland, drew attention to the dangers of resource depletion in its report *The Limits to Growth*. A year later, the economist E. F. Schumacher published a widely read book, *Small is Beautiful*, which challenged many of the basic assumptions of modern economies.

Sustainability poses a massive challenge to building design. Buildings use around half the world's energy and are therefore major contributors to the carbon-based gases that are thought to be responsible for global warming. In addition to the energy used in running a building, assessments of the building's overall footprint now

"Sustainability is the major issue of our time with a direct impact on architecture."

include the energy needed to construct it (including, for example, the travel distances of tradesmen and others); the energy embodied in its materials through the processes of extraction, processing, manufacture, and delivery to site; and the sustainability of the materials themselves. In the developed world, building regulations are being almost continuously updated to ensure compliance with good practice, but while these are effective with new buildings, a major source of problems worldwide—existing buildings—remains intractable.

It is now widely recognized that ecological sustainability needs to be married to social and economic sustainability, although the tension between the advocacy of sustainable development and the belief in free-market economics predicated on unlimited growth is rarely discussed,

let alone addressed, by governments. Given the threat of global warming, sustainability is clearly the major issue of our time with a direct impact on architecture. But while it is changing the way architects work, and the technical detailing of buildings, its impact on the expressive qualities of architecture, beyond overtly "ecological" buildings that wear their green credentials like a hair shirt, is still hard to discern. ∎

"An assault on horizontal planes, vertical walls, and a structural grid."

Blossoming at the end of a street in Bilbao, the Frank Gehry-designed Guggenheim Museum epitomizes the complex, sometimes seemingly chaotic, forms typical of so-called architectural Deconstruction.

Destroying the dream of pure form

IDEA № 96
DECONSTRUCTION

The most obvious challenge to orthodoxy presented by Deconstructionist projects was their shared assault on such familiar norms as horizontal floor planes, vertical walls, and a regular structural grid. Many appeared to teeter on the edge of collapse, and rather than deriving from a functional program uses for space were allocated later.

TOP: With its colliding grids, unfinished "scaffolding," and fragmented reconstruction of the Armory towers that occupied a nearby site until their demolition in 1958, Peter Eisenman's Wexner Center for the Visual Arts at Ohio State University (1983–89) was among the earliest built examples of Deconstructivist architecture.

ABOVE: Daniel Libeskind's award-winning design for the Jewish Museum in Berlin is based on a complex reading of the site and of the city's Jewish history.

Expounded by the French philosopher Jacques Derrida in *Of Grammatology*, Deconstruction proposed a radical critique of Western philosophy by challenging the privileging of speech over writing and exposing the power relations that underpin the familiar binary distinctions—form/content, nature/culture, thought/perception, theory/practice, male/female—that it frequently invokes. By exposing the "systematic structure of hierarchical privilege" implicit in these oppositions, whereby one side occupies a "sovereign" or "governing" power, Deconstruction sought to show that the subjugated position—the "other"—was equally necessary, and that fresh creative possibilities were opened up by exploring the new space for thought between the two.

Among the first to attempt to apply Derrida's complex ideas in architecture were Peter Eisenman and Bernard Tschumi. Invoking terms such as "de-composition," "decentering," and "discontinuity' they sought to undermine Classical and Modernist norms. In Eisenman's Wexner Center for the Visual Arts at Ohio State University (1982–83, left top) the prevailing order of the campus grid was "destabilized" by projecting a new axis derived from the Mercator grid used to map the earth. A brick armory long-demolished was rebuilt, undermining an historical reading of the site; a white steel grid-structure that penetrates the complex questions the idea of completion. In Tschumi's Parc de la Villette in Paris,

the entire project was conceived as an "incomplete building" and the familiar idea of meaning as derived from programmed use was challenged by scattering a grid of bright red "follies" across the site and assigning uses to them arbitrarily.

Eisenman and Tschumi were two of the seven architects featured in *Deconstructivist Architecture*, an exhibition organized by Philip Johnson and Mark Wigley at New York's Museum of Modern Art in 1988. This conflated the idea of Deconstruction with a burgeoning interest in the work of the Russian avant-garde of the 1920s—conveniently, if inaccurately, grouped under the term Constructivism—apparent in the work of participants, such as Rem Koolhaas, Zaha Hadid, and Tschumi, and marginal to that of others, notably Frank Gehry.

Increasingly in recent architecture sites and buildings have been seen as inscribed with multiple layers of meaning. The most celebrated and all-pervasive application of such ideas can be seen in Daniel Libeskind's Jewish Museum in Berlin (left bottom), whose fragmented forms were derived from the layering of several geometric systems, including a distorted Star of David and multiple axes that connect the addresses of Jewish families murdered in the Holocaust. ■

The city compacted into a single building

IDEA № 97

BIGNESS

In 1994 the Dutch architect Rem Koolhaas, founder and principal of the Office for Metropolitan Architecture (OMA), wrote that "In a landscape of disarray, disassembly, dissociation, disclamation, the attraction of Bigness is its potential to reconstruct the Whole, resurrect the Real, reinvent the collective, reclaim maximum possibility."

He saw Bigness as working outside the urban grain to create largely self-sufficient and self-serving mini-cities in a single building. The site was typically treated as a *tabula rasa* and the vast amount of accommodation and diverse uses were unconstrained by traditional architectural systems of order such as a column **grid**. Apparently contextless sites were often found on ex-urban land close to major highways or urban locations from which traces of past occupation were erased by comprehensive demolition and the re-organization of infrastructure.

The following year Koolhaas published his treatise on Bigness. Entitled *S, M, L, XL* (derived from clothes sizes), the first edition became a collector's item. His argument revolved around the idea that as a result of the past 150 years of activity within architecture and the market economy an extra-large scale of operation had emerged that attempts to incorporate multiple uses within a single spatial shell at vast, mega-proportions. Such projects, he argued, cannot be dealt with using traditional architectural ideas and techniques of spatial organization, and he called for a method of seeing, and acting, suited to this new scale—hence "Bigness," a new urbanism of the super-large.

For Koolhaas, Bigness, with all its implications for traditional cities, is an inevitable product of consumer capitalism, an uncontrollable condition that demands that the architect find new ways of negotiating its labyrinthine complexities. Projects such as major transportation interchanges, hubs, and commercial centers are treated by Koolhaas using the Bigness approach. OMA's Zeebrugge Sea Terminal, and more recently the China Central Television building in Beijing, demonstrate this by bringing together multiple functions within one vast spatial perimeter and devising an architectural approach to the overall formal qualities, most obviously in their distinctive shapes and massing, but also in their intellectual conception: Koolhaas describes a "regime of complexity," whereby the elements of the program interact in a generative way, producing new possibilities and events within the same shell.

Koolhaas did not see Bigness as a prescriptive manifesto, rather as identifying possibilities within the framework of activities taking place at this new scale. Implementation of many of these ideas in existing urban fabrics, new-build locations in the Middle East, vast, interiorized shopping malls in the U.S., and in other projects of super-scaled banality, however, proved less than satisfactory. They were analyzed in "The Harvard Project on the City," and in the first published text from this, *Harvard Design School Guide to Shopping*, Koolhaas wrote that "like a hurricane, globalization is rearranging the features of architecture. Architects now work in contexts, climates, and environments they know nothing about"—and as a result create what he calls "junkspace." "We have built more than all previous generations together," he observes, "but... we do not leave pyramids." ∎

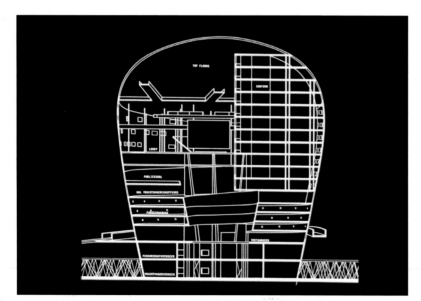

The 1989 competition design for the Zeebrugge Sea Terminal by OMA/Rem Koolhaas was an early, multi-use project that contributed to Koolhaas's ideas on the "Extra Large" scale explored in his influential 1995 book S,M,L,XL.

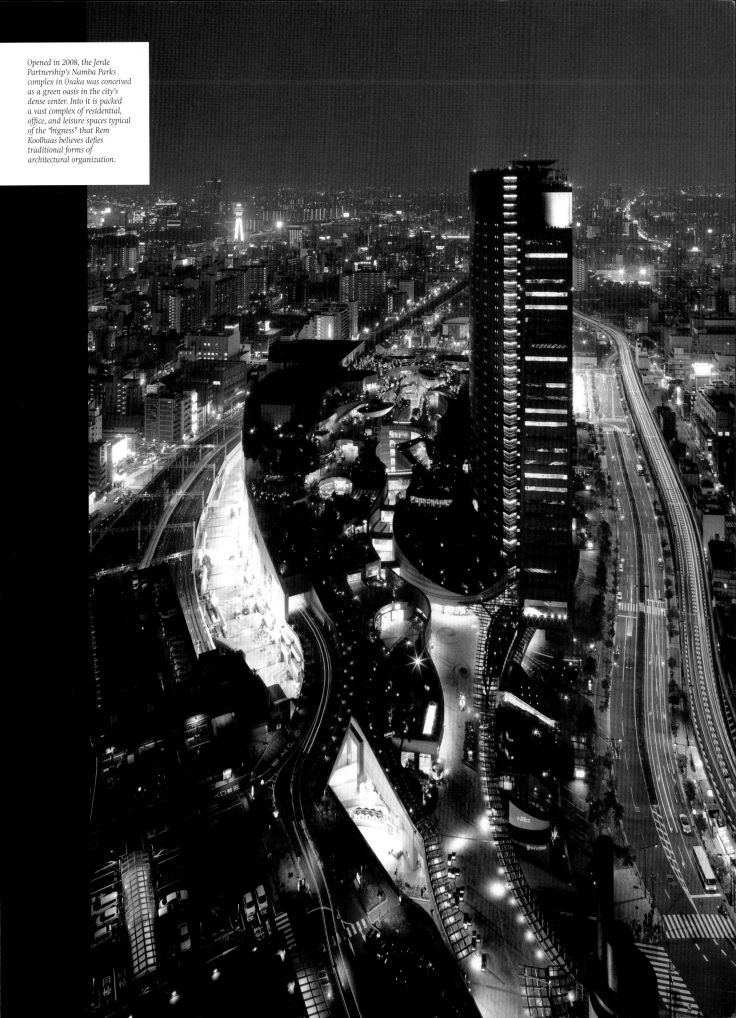

Opened in 2008, the Jerde Partnership's Namba Parks complex in Osaka was conceived as a green oasis in the city's dense center. Into it is packed a vast complex of residential, office, and leisure spaces typical of the "bigness" that Rem Koolhaas believes defies traditional forms of architectural organization.

Rem Koolhaas's Seattle Public Library, completed in 2004, is enclosed by folded plates of structural steel and glass that give few clues about its internal spatial organization.

Forms like fabric

FOLD

The Copenhagen Harbor Bath (2003) by PLOT architects was conceived as a continuous surface that starts as "ground" and is then folded to create a new public realm and enclose changing and other facilities.

The familiar word "fold" has recently taken center stage in an approach to architectural form that exploits the capacity of **computer-aided design** and manufacturing systems to create what the leading American exponent of digital architecture, Greg Lynn, calls "intricate assemblages."

While folded forms undoubtedly owe something of their popularity to the recent work of Frank Gehry, who is fascinated by the luxuriant folded fabrics seen in many eighteenth-century portraits, they are generated in very different ways. Gehry works like a sculptor, shaping a physical model that is handed over to technicians to be represented digitally by laser-scanning—the resulting "cloud of points" can then be developed as a digital Building Information Model and used to fabricate components using CADCAM systems. Digital designers, on the other hand, create forms using software that works upward from the parts.

At the theoretical level, the fascination with folding is indebted to a fiendishly difficult body of theory developed by the French philosopher Gilles Deleuze in his book *The Fold: Leibniz and the Baroque* (1988 in French, English translation 1993). Deleuze's idea of the fold (*le pli*) was based on Leibniz's concept of monads, which the great German philosopher-mathematician argued were to the metaphysical realm what atoms are to the physical/phenomenal world. Its use in the digital world is, not surprisingly, both more specific and technical, reflecting a wider interest in compositional practices involving weaving, folding, and joining that have led to what Lynn sees as a form of "digital Gothic." These slightly predated the software that is now used to generate folded forms, but it is undoubtedly the digital capability that has facilitated the dissemination of the approach.

The computer programs involved—known as spline-based packages—use **parametric** curves or "splines" to approximate complex, intricate shapes through a process known as curve fitting (the term "spline" derives from the flexible drawing tools formerly used by naval architects to draw the smooth curves typical of ships' hulls). The fascination with intricately folded forms also reflects a broader interest in the compositional and spatial complexity made possible by the ability of CAD systems to permit the intricate interlinking of diverse elements to create structures in which, to quote Lynn again, the "variation of the part is not reducible to the structure of the whole"—a key concept of the "systems theory" that originated in the 1960s.

Visually, folded forms appear voluptuous and homogeneous at a distance; a striking contrast to the formal incoherence of the heterogeneous mechanical parts from which they are fabricated. Folding can therefore be seen as a way of working that sits between the macro and micro scales, producing intricate compositions that reflect new technologies and modes of digitally based architectural production. Against the mechanical repetition of mass production typical of the first Industrial Revolution, folded forms are seen by their proponents as a semi-biological form of "intricate machine" production. And, as in earlier versions of **additive architecture**, this is used to generate complex variety and difference "from the bottom up" in a manner that purports to reflect the development of natural **organisms**. ∎

Completed in 2010, ten years after the original competition entry, Zaha Hadid's MAXXI: Museum of Twenty-First Century Arts in Rome was designed as a manifesto for "Parametricism," which aims to develop complex systems of order to organize and reflect the increasing complexity of the institutions and life of our network society.

"A particular 'style' is embedded in the digital code and graphical interface used."

Complex forms of the computer age

IDEA № 99

PARAMETRIC DESIGN

An increasing number of architects are now turning to parametric software that allows them to specify and repeatedly change relationships between various parameters in the features of a design. It has resulted in an architecture of previously unimagined forms.

Such programs are analogous to a conventional spreadsheet: by storing the mathematical relationships between the various features of a design, they allow elements to be changed. The whole model can then "regenerate" in much the same way that a spreadsheet recalculates numerical changes.

Parametric design originated in the aerospace and automotive industries as a means of designing complex curved forms to meet aerodynamic and other criteria. Conventional computer-aided design visualization techniques used in architecture do not allow a three-dimensional building model to be modified interactively.

The creation of a non-trivial parametric design model is demanding, requiring skills in computer programming, mathematics, and logic that are not part of most architects' education. To make matters worse for students eager to emulate the alluring, parametrically generated images that are increasingly familiar in magazines, each of the most popular commercial software systems uses a different approach to generating models.

Although parametric methods are most commonly associated with complex, fluid forms whose generative logic may not be obvious to the observer, as for example in the recent work of Zaha Hadid (opposite), they are also being used to explore sophisticated approaches to ecologically and environmentally responsive design. A pioneer in this area, much of whose work was undertaken before the word "parametric" was in common usage, is Ralph Knowles, whose concept of the "solar envelope" of a city or settlement used simple parametric techniques to maximize insolation.

In practice, parametric design is closely linked to the capabilities of increasingly sophisticated CADCAM techniques that facilitate the economical manufacture of numerous complex and often unique components. The recent work of Frank Gehry would be impossible without these, and the complex aerodynamic form and spiraling light wells of Foster and Partners' Swiss Re Tower in London (above) and the swelling glass roof of the Great Court at the British Museum (also by Foster) were both designed and manufactured in this way.

By describing the logic and intent behind a design proposal, rather than just one specific manifestation of them, parametric tools drastically reduce the time required to explore successive iterations of a design. Like the development of **orthographic**

For the Swiss Re Tower in London—generally known as "the Gherkin"—Foster and Partners used fluid dynamics software to compute the optimal profile and then converted this into a dynamic parametric model to control the detailed building geometry. What seems to be curved glass was automatically converted into planar elements whose shape and location would automatically update with every design change to the overall geometry.

projection, its implications are far-reaching and Patrick Schumacher, a partner in Zaha Hadid Architects, has coined the term "Parametricism" as the name of a putative new movement in architecture.

Both Foster and Partners and Frank Gehry—and doubtless others—now employ computer programmers to work as part of design teams, highlighting a major issue raised by the current generation of parametric software—namely, that a particular "style" is effectively embedded in the digital code and graphical interface they use. Working parametrically, all programming decisions are design decisions, and architects—understood as practices if not necessarily individuals—are going to need a new range of skills fully to master these powerful new techniques. ∎

Artfully familiar design

EVERYDAY

The term "the everyday" has come to embrace two seemingly contradictory concerns: the conviction that architects are becoming distant professionals on the one hand, and on the other a highly aestheticized determination to make an architecture that looks artfully familiar and "everyday."

Interest in the "everyday" is a widespread preoccupation among young architects and theorists in the early twenty-first century, and can be traced back to the emergence of pop culture and social activism in the 1950s and 1960s. In response to the former, architects such as Alison and Peter Smithson in England became fascinated by the consumer products of the U.S., while later—in his book *Complexity and Contradiction in Architecture* published in 1966—Robert Venturi declared the familiar Main Street of U.S. towns "almost all right" and later went on to extol the virtues of the Las Vegas strip (see pp.170–72).

Faced by the challenge of postwar reconstruction, the Smithsons rejected the slab- and point-block models that were being widely adopted in favor of what they christened "streets in the

sky." These were inspired, in part, by widely admired photographs by Nigel Henderson of children playing in the streets of London's East End. A similar concern with working-class culture soon led younger, politically committed thinkers to question the value of architecture, as conventionally understood, as a means of "solving" such problems. Echoing the critique of professions advanced by Ivan Illich and others, they argued that architects, expensively educated to graduate level, were inevitably separated—in terms of education, privilege, and class—from the people for whom they design. In response, the **community architecture** movement of the 1970s promoted people's participation in design and (self-) building, and cast the architect as an enabler familiar with the planning system, building regulations, and other statutory and practical requirements.

The recent revival of interest in the everyday received a substantial stimulus with the publication in 1997 of a collection of papers edited by Steven Berke and Deborah Harris. Entitled *Architecture of the Everyday*, its various contributors explored connections between professionalized high architecture and everyday building. Espousing the virtues of the ordinary, banal, and quotidian, the book represented the ideals of a growing number of architects keen to escape the cycles of consumption and fashion that, under the stylistic **Postmodernism** of the 1980s, had threatened to reduce architecture to a stylish fad. In its place, the authors argued the case for buildings that are unmonumental and antiheroic, and grounded in the familiar routines and environments of daily life.

Inspired by such writings, by contemporary art and photography dealing with similar themes, and by the work of an earlier generation epitomized by Alison and Peter Smithson, some architects also began to look more artfully for an everyday aesthetic—hence, for example, the work of the London-based practice Sergison Bates, who came to attention with the design of a public house in Walsall and a pair of semi-detached houses in Stevenage, and whose more recent projects in London espouse a fascination with the city's ubiquitous yellow-gray stock-brick walls. ∎

Glossary

art nouveau
Art nouveau (known as *Jugendstil* in German-speaking countries) was an anti-academic style embracing all the arts that looked to nature as a source of inspiration.

apse
A semicircular recess covered with a hemispherical vault; in Christian churches an apse may also be polygonal and is frequently used to terminate the east end of the building.

Baroque
A style characterized by dynamic movement that flourished in the later seventeenth and early eighteenth centuries. It was promoted by the Roman Catholic Counter-Reformation.

bill of quantities
A document used to estimate the costs of a building that specifies the types, quality, and quantities of all materials needed for its construction.

building information model (BIM)
A three-dimensional computer model of a building that coordinates all aspects of its design—spatial organization, structure, components, building services, etc.

CADCAM
Acronym for Computer-Aided Design/Computer-Aided Manufacturing, in which the digital model of a building may also be used to generate files that control machines making bespoke components.

came
A lead bar used to join small pieces of glass to create a large leaded light.

cartouche
Originally a term used to describe a rectangular frame containing a royal name in Egyptian hieroglyphs, later extended to similar framing of motifs in Classical decoration.

Classical
In architecture, "Classical" is generally used to refer to a style derived from ancient Greece and Rome that was revived in the Renaissance and became the basis of the academic form of architecture widely taught in schools of architecture well into the twentieth century.

clerestory
Originally applied to the upper story of Roman basilicas or Christian churches, now commonly used to denote a continuous run of glazing between wall and ceiling.

console
A type of projecting bracket or corbel, typically with a scroll-shaped profile.

Corinthian
The third of the three Greek Orders, its column is characterized by a slender, fluted shaft and elaborate capital incorporating stylized leaves.

Doric
The oldest of the Greek Orders, with a sturdy, fluted column and unelaborated capital.

enfilade
A sequence of interlinked rooms, generally with their doors aligned to form a long visual axis through them.

entablature
The horizontal upper part of a Classical Order, comprising the architrave that links the columns, the frieze, and a projecting cornice.

Formalism
The belief that a building's artistic value resides entirely in its forms, considered independent of use, meaning, or context.

Functionalism
The belief that a building's forms can and should be determined entirely by their purpose—which may be practical, structural, or environmental.

geodesic
In architecture "geodesic" refers to a form of dome invented by Richard Buckminster Fuller and based on a network of great circles.

Golden Ratio/Golden Mean
An "ideal" proportion for a rectangle in which A:B and A+B:A are equal; the resulting ratio is an irrational number—1:1.61803...

Gothic
A style of architecture that originated in twelfth-century France, survived into the sixteenth, and was revived in the nineteenth century, characterized structurally by pointed arches and vaults.

helical
A smooth curve in space, familiar from screws and so-called "spiral" staircases. (Properly used, the term spiral refers to a continuously expanding two-dimensional curve.)

Ionic
The second of the Classical Orders, characterized by a column with a fluted shaft and a capital with distinctive spiraling volutes.

Mannerist
Exponent or characteristic expression of a style based on deliberate distortion of the Classical style of architecture.

materiality
The material qualities of a building, widely used when these are seen as of particular importance to the architectural expression.

Modern/Modernist
Modern with a capital "M" is widely used to refer to the progressive architectural ideas that dominated the years 1920–39, while Modernist refers to an exponent of the cluster of radical movements that diffused through all the arts in the first half of the twentieth century.

mullion
A vertical subdivision of a window opening.

nave
The central space of a basilica, or of the Christian churches based on the basilican form, generally flanked by aisles.

Neoclassicism
A style advocating a return to strict Classical principles that began in the mid-eighteenth century as a reaction to the florid Rococo architecture of the day.

new urbanism
A term used in the U.K. and U.S. to refer to the advocacy of traditional, often Classical, forms of urban design.

orthogonal (geometry)
A system of formal organization based entirely

on lines and planes arranged in parallel or at 90 degrees to each other.

palazzo
The Italian word for "palace," but used far more widely to refer to a grand house, home of an institution, or even a large block of apartments.

parti
A French term used in the Beaux-Arts style to refer to the basic organizing idea for a building.

pendentive
A curved surface that connects a circular or elliptical dome to a square or rectangular space below.

piano nobile/piano rustica
In Italian the word *piano* means floor: the "noble" floor denotes the main (usually second) floor where the principal apartments of a large house or palazzo would be located, while the "rustic" floor refers to the ground floor which, in Classical buildings, is often treated with rusticated stone.

pilaster
A slightly projecting, generally flattened, column built into a wall.

planar
Literally "having the character of a plane," generally used to refer to the treatment of walls, floors, and ceiling that emphasizes their abstract character as (typically) rectangular planes.

Rococo
An ornate, florid version of the Baroque style that emanated from the French court and flourished in the mid-eighteenth century.

rustication
A form of masonry featuring rough surface and exaggerated joints, typically used on ground floors to suggest strength and security.

spline
Derived from a draftsman's tool for drawing curves, the term spline now generally refers to the form of curves that are most easily manipulated using CAD software.

stratification
Literally "building up in layers" the term stratification is generally used in architecture to suggest an emphasis on the buildup of floors and other horizontal elements in a building.

thermal bridges/cold bridges
Uninsulated, solid elements—such as columns in the wall plane or projecting beams—that could conduct heat from inside to outside.

thermal flywheel
The capacity of walls, floors, or other solid elements of a building to absorb heat energy and then release it when the interior cools down, helping to reduce cooling and heating requirements.

tracery
The complex networks of slender stone elements that support the glass in Gothic windows.

transept
The area, generally found in church architecture, set at right angles to the nave and projecting on each side to form the crossbar of a Latin-cross plan.

transom
The horizontal, transverse beam in a frame, most commonly used to refer to the subdivision of window or door openings.

truth to materials
The doctrine that a building's structure and form should follow from the "honest" use of materials that respects their "nature" or properties.

Vitruvian triad
The most famous short definition of architecture posited by the Roman architect Vitruvius: *commoditas*, *firmitas*, and *venustas* in Latin; commodity, firmness, and delight in Sir Henry Wotton's famous English translation.

Further reading

General histories of architecture

Sir Banister Fletcher. *Sir Banister Fletcher's A History of Architecture*. Ed. by Dan Cruickshank. Oxford: Architectural Press, 20th ed., 1996.
Regularly updated for more than a century, this monumental, profusely illustrated book remains the most comprehensive account of world architecture in English.

Spiro Kostof. *History of Architecture: Settings and Rituals*. Oxford, New York: Oxford University Press, 2007.

Vincent Scully. *Architecture: The Natural and the Manmade*. New York: St. Martin's Press, 1991.

Modern architecture

Leonardo Benevolo. *History of Modern Architecture. Vol.1: The Tradition of Modern Architecture. Vol.2: The Modern Movement*. London: Routledge & Kegan Paul, 1971.
A monumental account of modern architecture up to 1939, situating twentieth-century developments in a broad historical context.

Alan Colquhoun. *Modern Architecture*. Oxford, New York: Oxford University Press, 2002.
A recent, highly readable reevaluation of the first half-century of Modern architecture.

Peter Collins. *Changing Ideals in Modern Architecture, 1750–1950*. Montreal : McGill-Queens University Press, 2nd ed., 1998.
A classic study that was among the first to set the ideas of Modern architecture in an extended historical perspective.

William Curtis. *Modern Architecture Since 1900*. London: Phaidon, 3rd ed., 1996.
Having expanded to almost 800 pages Curtis's book can appear daunting, but it remains one of the best and most readable accounts of twentieth-century architecture.

Kenneth Frampton. *Modern Architecture: A Critical History*. London; New York: Thames & Hudson, 4th ed., 2007.
First published in 1980, this is still one of the best compact histories of modern architecture—although Frampton's critical perspective was criticized by some professional historians.

Sigfried Giedion. *Space, Time and Architecture: The Growth of a New Tradition*. Cambridge, MA; London: Harvard University Press, 5th rev. and enlarged ed., 2008.
As the Secretary of CIAM (The International Congresses of Modern Architecture), Giedion was at the heart of the development of Modern architecture. Although now criticized for its partisan approach and selective use of history, it remains a seminal study.

Henry Russell Hitchcock and Philip Johnson. *The International Style*. New foreword by Philip Johnson. New York: W.W. Norton, 1996.
Published in 1932 to accompany the New York Museum of Modern Art's landmark exhibition of new architecture in Europe and the Americas, this book proved hugely influential in promoting—to the annoyance of some of its exponents—the idea of Modern architecture as an international "style."

Nikolaus Pevsner. *Pioneers of Modern Design: From William Morris to Walter Gropius*. Introduction by Richard Weston. New Haven, CT; London: Yale University Press, 2005.
An expanded edition with color illustrations of Pevsner's classic, hugely influential 1936 book that constructed and popularized the idea of the "Modern Movement" in architecture.

Richard Weston. *Key Buildings of the Twentieth Century: Plans, Sections and Elevations*. London: Laurence King, 2nd ed., 2010.
Similar in format to the present book, this offers an overview of modern architecture through short, illustrated essays and specially prepared drawings.

Richard Weston. *Modernism*. London: Phaidon, 1996.
An accessible, wide-ranging account of Modernism, focusing on architecture but including graphic and industrial design and key innovations in painting.

Architectural theory and criticism

Reyner Banham. *Theory and Design in the First Machine Age*. Oxford: Butterworth Architecture, 1994.
Reprint of the classic 1960 text that offered a detailed, historically informed critique of Modern architecture, drawing attention to then largely

forgotten movements such as the Italian futurists.

Kenneth Frampton. *Studies in Tectonic Culture: the Poetics of Construction in Nineteenth- and Twentieth-century Architecture*. Cambridge, MA: MIT Press, 1995.
An ambitious critique that attempts to redress what Frampton sees as the over-emphasis on space at the expense of constructional expression in recent architecture.

Charles Jencks. *The Language of Postmodern Architecture*. London: Academy Editions, 2nd enlarged ed., 1978.
Jencks's book famously declared the "death" of Modern architecture and launched the idea of a Postmodernism style dominated by ideas of language, communication, and symbolism.

Le Corbusier, tr. By Frederick Etchells. *Towards a New Architecture*. Oxford: Architectural Press, 1989.
One of the most influential books on architecture ever written, first published in French in 1923.

Charles W. Moore, Gerald Allen, and Donlyn Lyndon. *The Place of Houses*. Berkeley: University of California Press, 2000.
First published in 1974 this remains an enjoyable, informative introduction to architecture written for a general audience.

Juhani Pallasmaa. *The Eyes of the Skin: Architecture and the Senses*. Chichester: Wiley-Academy. 2nd ed., 2005.
Widely read in schools of architecture, Pallasmaa's book offers a stimulating critique of what he sees as the over-emphasis on the visual in contemporary architecture.

Steen Eiler Rasmussen. *Experiencing Architecture*, Cambridge, Mass: MIT Press, 2nd ed., 1962.
A classic account of the experiential qualities of architecture, first published in 1959 but still widely recommended as an introduction to the subject.

Colin Rowe. *The Mathematics of the Ideal Villa and Other Essays*. Cambridge, MA; London: MIT Press, 1976.
A collection of revisionist essays by one of the most influential architectural writers of his generation; the title essay provocatively compared villas by Le Corbusier and Palladio.

Vitruvius Pollio, tr. by Richard Schofield. *On*

Architecture. London: Penguin, 2009.
The most influential book in architectural history, also known as the *Ten Books of Architecture*, Vitruvius's text was the foundation of the Renaissance revival of Classical architecture.

Gottfried **Semper** tr. by Harry Francis Mallgrave and Wolfgang Herrmann. *The Four Elements of Architecture and Other Writings*. Cambridge: Cambridge University Press, 1989.
Semper's *Four Elements* was a seminal text of the nineteenth century and this book—which includes an extended introduction by Mallgrave—is the best introduction to his ideas.

John Ruskin, edited and abridged by J. G. Links. *The Stones of Venice*. London: Pallas Athene in conjunction with Ostara, 2001.
Contains Ruskin's account of "The Nature of Gothic," one of the essential texts of the nineteenth century.

Eugène-Emmanuel Viollet-le-Duc. *The Architectural Theory of Viollet-Le-Duc*. Readings and commentary edited by M. F. Hearn. Cambridge, MA: MIT Press, 1990.
A good introduction to the ideas of the most important architectural theorist since Alberti.

Richard Weston. *Materials, Form and Architecture*. London: Laurence King, 2003.
A cultural rather than technical exploration of changing attitudes to the use of materials in architecture.

Rudolf Wittkower. *Architectural Principles in the Age of Humanism*. London: Academy, 1988.
That rare thing: a serious piece of architectural writing that, through its exploration of proportional systems, exerted a major influence on a generation of practicing architects.

Monographs

Anthony Grafton. *Leon Battista Alberti*: Master Builder of the Italian Renaissance. London: Penguin, 2002.

Richard Weston. *Alvar Aalto*. London: Phaidon, 1995.

Philip Jodidio. *Ando: Complete Works*. Cologne, Los Angeles: Taschen, 2004.

Peter Blundell Jones. *Gunnar Asplund*. London: Phaidon, 2006.

Pieter Singelenberg. *H.P. Berlage: Idea and Style: The Quest for Modern Architecture*. Utrecht: Haentjens Dekker and Gumbert, 1972.

Vincent Ligtelijn. *Aldo van Eyck: Works*. Basel; Boston: Birkhäuser, 1999.

Arnulf Lüchinger, ed. Herman **Hertzberger**. *Buildings and Projects*. The Hague: Arch-Edition, 1987.

David Brownlee. *Louis I. Kahn: In the Realm of Architecture*. New York: Rizzoli, 1991.

William Curtis. *Le Corbusier: Ideas and Forms*. London: Phaidon, 1995.

Ralf Bock. *Adolf Loos: Works and Projects*. Milan: Skira, 2007.

David A. Spaeth. *Mies van der Rohe*. London: Architectural Press, 1985.

Robert Tavernor. *Palladio and Palladianism*. London: Thames & Hudson, 1991.

Neil **Levine**. *The Architecture of Frank Lloyd Wright*. Princeton, N.J.: Princeton University Press, 1996.

Richard Weston. *Utzon. Inspiration, Vision, Architecture*. Hellerup: Edition Bløndal, 2002.

Index

Page numbers in **bold** refer to picture captions

Published in 2011 by
Laurence King Publishing Ltd
361–373 City Road
London EC1V 1LR

e-mail: enquiries@laurenceking.com
www.laurenceking.com

A catalogue record for this book is available
from the British Library.

ISBN: 978-1-85669-732-3

Design: Two Sheds Design
Picture research: Claire Gouldstone
Senior editor: Peter Jones
Printed in China

The author would like to thank Sam Austin,
Ed Wainwright, and Chloe Sambell for their
help with the research for this book and also the
various colleagues and friends with whom it was
discussed informally from listing to writing.

The image on p.2 shows the Louvre Museum at
night with I. M. Pei's glass and steel pyramid
in the foreground.

Picture credits